D0813455

# THE
# GREAT
# STAGFLATION
## INVESTMENT STRATEGIES
# FOR A NEW ERA

### PHIL TAYLOR-GUCK

# R<sup>e</sup>think

First published in Great Britain in 2021 by Rethink Press
(www.rethinkpress.com)

Disclaimer
The views expressed in this book do not constitute
financial advice. The investment ideas discussed
should never be used without first assessing your own
financial situation and consulting a qualified financial
advisor. Neither the author nor the publisher can be
held responsible for any losses that may result from
investments made after reading this book.

# Contents

# Introduction

The feedback from my first book, *Gold Rush 2020*,[1] taught me a valuable lesson. While many people say they know all they need to know about the financial world, this is not actually true. The majority of us tend to bumble along, thinking we've just about got a handle on things and, in any case, we can rely on the experts to make sure things are OK. Let's park the fact that it is probably quite foolish to rely on politicians and central bankers to keep on top of things, since the majority of past financial crises have been entirely man-made. The point is, we all have a responsibility to make sure we understand economics, on both a personal and a broader scale. Money plays such a vital role in all of our lives. We need to get to grips with what is going on, in order to make the best decisions for ourselves and our families.

A great deal of the success of my first book was down to the way that I simplified the arguments around gold's role as the ultimate insurance policy, particularly at times of financial crisis. Since that book was published (in 2019), the world has been plunged into its biggest crisis of generations, thanks to the COVID-19 pandemic. Initially, in the face of widespread uncertainty, the markets slumped. Billions were wiped off investments, almost overnight. There was a (remarkably rapid) recovery of sorts. Indeed, some sectors of the stock market were positively buoyant even in the early days of the first lockdown. By early 2021, with vaccines being rolled out across the globe, the talk switched to returning to normal in every aspect of our lives. The expectation was that everyone would return to exactly the same routines as before and the rest of the markets would make a complete recovery. It is my strong contention that this will not be the case and not just because the coronavirus will be a big presence in our lives for some years to come, regardless of the success of the vaccination programme. There will most likely be some dark economic times ahead. Indeed, all the signs point to a lengthy period of stagflation, an economic phenomenon that we haven't seen since the 1970s.

It would be very easy, and most likely quite comforting, to dismiss the possibility of the harsh realities of stagflation. *No politician has mentioned this,* you may say. *Economists don't talk about it.* Well, they wouldn't, would they? It is hardly a vote winner to admit that, following one of the most difficult years of most people's lives, there could be tougher times to follow. Similarly, prior to the 1970s, economists insisted that there was no possible way stagflation even existed. This is why I have returned to my keyboard to write *The Great Stagflation*. I wanted to lay out the reasons why I believe we are entering extremely uncertain economic times. Crucially, I wanted to highlight the ways that individuals can help themselves and secure their own finances. While stagflation will cause widespread damage to an already fragile global economy, there is no reason why your savings and lifestyle should take a massive hit. As I laid out in *Gold Rush 2020*, gold is a good hedge at times of economic collapse and that will be the case now. However, other strategies are worthy of consideration too.

Getting through the post-COVID period will require some changes. Number one among these is to be prepared for change: there will be change. There is no such thing as 'normal'. (Not to mention that your normal may be very different from my normal, or indeed anyone else's.) Equally important is to be alert to the early signs of stagflation and to prepare strategies to withstand it. This book will explain how.

# ONE

# Welcome To The Great Stagflation

Fortune favours the prepared, or so the saying goes. Yet, despite the dire start to the 2020s, thanks to the COVID-19 pandemic, not to mention Brexit and a highly polarised and volatile political environment worldwide, few are ready for the personal and financial impact of what is forecast to come next. Right now all the signs point to our entering an unprecedented economic environment: a period of Great Stagflation.

The majority have barely even heard of stag-flation and, of those who have, most won't understand it properly, and still fewer know how to prepare for it. It is, however, something that cannot be ignored because, if the economy moves in this direction, it will have a profound impact on all of our financial futures.

For the uninitiated, stagflation is the worst possible macroeconomic combo: the simulta-neous occurrence of a stagnating jobs market and high inflation; or, more specifically, high unemployment at the same time as rising prices. On a purely human level, it is a nightmare scenario for people who lose their jobs while also facing a markedly higher cost of living. At the same time, it presents an almost impossible dilemma for policymakers, since actions that might be taken to lower inflation may push up unemployment, adding to the problem.

For many decades, most economic models didn't dwell on such an extreme eventuality. Indeed, stagnation was once viewed as an *impossible* economic theory. Economists focused their attention on the 'or' side of the and/or model when it came to unemployment and inflation. They said we can have high unemployment *or* high inflation, but never both at the same time. To illustrate the naysayers' train of thought, let's take Keynesian economics as an example. According to this theory, inflation is a product of an over-heated economy. Economic prosperity and growth lead to high levels of employment, which in turn drive up wages. Better wages create a demand for better standards of living, which drives demand for goods and services and, as a consequence, prices rise thanks to the impact of supply and demand. This also means wages, the primary costs of production, are higher and that squeezes profit margins. Factories and retailers raise prices to offset this, which in turn encourages workers to demand higher wages so they can buy all the things they need and want. It's a classic inflationary spiral. Traditionally, high unemployment can be relied upon to have the opposite effect. A harsh jobs market saps demand for goods and sends prices downwards. So, there you have it. Classical thinking would have us believe that high inflation and low growth are mutually exclusive.

The economists, as it transpired, were wrong and were roundly proved to be so in the 1970s where both the UK and the USA experienced a bruising period of stagflation. While the decade started promisingly, with record low unemployment thanks to a strong rise in postwar manufacturing, when things began to go wrong, they went downhill very quickly. Contrary to all the economic pronouncements, we experienced a mix of events that set the scene for stagflation. Nations around the world were hit by an oil crisis in the fall-out of the Yom Kippur War. Oil giant OPEC, which then controlled around 60% of the world's oil, abruptly stopped supplying the West. With oil prices soaring, firms rapidly laid off workers. Those individuals who were fortunate enough to stay in work saw their pay-slips shrinking in value because they couldn't keep pace with rocketing inflation. The impossible had become possible: stagflation had happened – growing unemployment had arrived at the same time prices were rising. In the UK, which was very badly impacted, the crippling combination quickly spiralled into widespread public unrest and anger, which then escalated into a series of national strikes.

By 1975, inflation had soared from the low single digits to around 24% – the highest level in decades.[2] To make matters worse, there seemed little consensus among the authorities on how best to deal with the advent of stagnation that no one seemed remotely prepared for. During the ensuing Winter of Discontent, when talks between the Labour government and unions broke down, everyone from rubbish collectors, to grave diggers, to nurses, came out on strike. The streets became lined with piles of rubbish, many dead went unburied and hospital systems broke down, leaving an enduring record of what happens when stagflation hits, vividly recorded in many photographs of the day.

It took a while for governments worldwide to come up with measures to curb the damaging fall-out from the first ever period of stagflation, but they did eventually get there. The approaches were varied, from raising interest rates to high levels to purposely induce a severe recession, to curtailing the flow of money, to enduring exceptionally high levels of unemployment. In each case, the political will to take what would ordinarily be extreme measures was strong, despite an already volatile domestic situation. This was because, while respective governments faced what was an entirely new set of circumstances, they understood that the longer stagflation was allowed to continue, the worse the long-term damage would be.

(What is interesting to note is that, while bad, the stagnation of the 1970s was not as bad as many people remember. Despite the powerful black-and-white images depicting riots and rubbish-strewn streets, the actual numbers are not as devastating as you might think. Taking the UK as an example, the 1970s were not the worst period for unemployment. Despite the chaos, unemployment never rose above 6% of working-age people. In the 1980s, it soared to 12%.[3] In other words, the stagflation of the 1970s was bad, but it could have been a lot worse.)

# The 2020s are nothing like the 1970s

Fast-forward half a century and economists aren't quite bold enough to say stagflation is impossible any more, but there are still a fair number of quite confident pronouncements that the right elements are not in place for that to happen. The 2020s are nothing like the 1970s, say the economists. The influencing factors are 180° different. To be fair, there is a certain amount of merit in this argument. Take oil as a case in point, since the Organization of the Petroleum Exporting Countries (OPEC) oil embargo was credited with triggering the 1970s stagnation. The oil situation is indeed nowhere near the same today. In fact, in April 2020 we saw the somewhat unusual situation of oil prices turning negative for the first time on record. Behind this phenomenon was slumping demand, thanks to restrictions on travel owing to lockdowns all over the globe in response to COVID-19, and oil producers running out of space to store the over-supply of crude. In a matter of hours, the cost of US crude oil crashed from $18 a barrel to -$38.

It's not just the oil situation that is different. The stagflation naysayers will point to the fact that there are currently no signs of rising inflation; and they'd be right. Within months of the start of the pandemic, most world economies were already plunged into significant recession, with low growth and low inflation. Demand was weak as governments tackled the debt building up through the pandemic and businesses and consumers remained cautious about spending. As well as hitting oil prices, the collapse in demand fed through to lower energy costs, all at the same time as a veritable deluge of offers from retailers desperate to clear pre-lockdown stock. As airlines, restaurants and leisure outfits reopened in between bouts of complete lockdown, there were numerous bargains on offer in a heavy run of discounting to encourage people to spend. Headline inflation rates were highly tipped to turn negative. Economic experts pointed out that there was no way of knowing how low inflation and growth could sink, either. If it turns out that the coronavirus had a very significant deflationary impact, it could push the world's economies into depression, which would be a new experience for almost everyone. The developed world has not experienced deflation on any significant scale since the 1930s. While there have been bouts of disinflation, which is basically a slowdown in inflation, there has been no actual deflation, in which prices and asset values fall. It would therefore be fair to say that, as long as the globe continues to battle the pandemic, deflation and low growth will remain very real threats.

But, let's leave the scenario to play out, because there is a real possibility that the slump in demand is the lull before the storm. While the circumstances of the early 2020s are entirely different from the ones that triggered the previous period of stagflation, there is a strong possibility that we are heading towards the same end point.

While scientists across the world were working long hours in a bid to find a COVID-19 vaccine, one-half of the conditions needed to create stagflation was steadily ticking up: unemployment. Six months into the pandemic, the unemployment rate in the UK rose to a near two-year high, as almost 750,000 jobs were recorded as being lost during this period.[4] The actual figures were believed to be much higher, since the recorded numbers did not take into account employees who have been furloughed and may never return to their previous workplace. Indeed, the Organisation for Economic Co-operation and Development (OECD) predicted the number of unemployed in the UK could hit 15% of the total working population. A slightly more optimistic scenario from the Office for Budget Responsibility (OBR) saw the unemployment rate peaking at around 10% in 2020, and returning to pre-coronavirus levels by 2022. But, before anyone begins to sigh with relief, it is worth noting that the OBR also released a bleaker forecast, predicting that unemployment numbers would peak at 13% in 2021, with 4 million out of work, and 6.3% still out of a job by 2024, well ahead of pre-crisis levels.[5] To put this into perspective, this would be the highest jobless rate since 1984, when unemployment peaked at 11.9%.[6] In 2019, the year before coronavirus arrived in the UK, the country was celebrating a record jobs market and unemployment at just 3.9%.[7]

Since the UK is still closely tied to the global economy, despite the trend towards decoupling ourselves via Brexit and other protectionist measures, it is worth noting that we are not alone when it comes to falling employment levels. Indeed, in some countries the situation is forecast to become a lot worse. One senior Federal Reserve official has predicted that unemployment in the USA could hit 30% in the months ahead.[8] James Bullard, president and CEO of the Federal Reserve Bank of St Louis, made this forecast in the wake of data showing US unemployment claims were growing faster than at any point during modern history. Worldwide, the International Labour Organization says the equivalent of more than 300 million full-time jobs were lost in the second quarter of 2020, once the billions of workers in the 'gig' economy were taken into account.[9] There can be no argument that the world is facing a period of very high unemployment.

OK, so what about the other half of the equation, inflation? This economic factor is very much tied in with the end of the pandemic.

The most optimistic forecasts assume that we will all happily return to normal once the series of stop-start lockdowns ends. It is a hopeful vision promoted by governments of different nations, supported by aggressive fiscal and monetary stimulus to stop economies from sliding into depression, thereby setting the stage for everyone to go back to life just as it used to be. In order for this somewhat rosy viewpoint to become true, all of us would need to be 100% sure that we could resume our former lives with as close to zero risk of catching COVID-19 as it is possible to achieve. For this to be the case, the vaccines would have to pretty much eradicate the disease *and* be administered to the entire global population, too. Without wishing to get too far into the realms of epidemiology, it is worth saying that this is quite a big ask. The challenge of orchestrating a rapid, effective and affordable worldwide vaccination programme is not for the faint-hearted.

Nevertheless, at some point a vaccine will achieve most of what it is supposed to do. What then? The widespread hope is that the pressures that caused the deflationary scenario will abate as the economy begins to reopen. Ideally, it will be an orderly event, with a steady and well-managed recovery. No government wants to be in a position where demand suddenly spikes, sending prices soaring. The expectation is that widespread unemployment and ongoing concerns over debt amassed through the pandemic should be sufficient to keep many consumers away from the shops. Yet there is a very real possibility that the wishes of policymakers won't come true. Consumers who have kept their wallets firmly closed throughout the pandemic will be eager to get back to 'normal'. The economy may well experience the full, explosive impact of pent-up demand. Assuming that, in the interim, the government continues to support incomes in some shape or form this urge to spend, spend, spend will spark a swift and significant inflationary spiral. Supply restrictions will further fuel this scenario because many firms have gone bust, or have spent months operating under rules that have limited their production capacity. Meanwhile, in order to keep people safe as the economy reopens, aeroplanes may still be required to fly with a reduced passenger load, restaurants and arts venues will only be able to accommodate a fraction of their pre-pandemic numbers and retailers may need to keep some sort of ongoing restriction on the number of people allowed in their stores. With a cap on the number of customers they can serve, businesses will need to raise their prices to stay profitable. Thus, even if there is no spike in demand, we will see higher prices.

Stagflation – high inflation and high unemployment – will have returned.

## Can it happen again?

There are many economists, bankers and government officials that will continue to believe this can't happen. Most likely, they will rebuff the very suggestion of stagflation by deploying many of the same arguments that were trotted out in the aftermath of the 2008/9 global financial crisis. The fear then was that the vast amount of money being created out of thin air by central banks via quantitative easing (QE) would see the sort of hyper-inflation not seen since 1920s Weimar Germany. As it turns out, these naysayers will tell you, the complete opposite happened. In fact, there have been widespread concerns over most of the past decade that inflation is *too low*, not too high. Unemployment has remained low also and any fears that a steady reduction in unemployment would encourage workers to pursue inflationary wage claims have proved entirely unfounded.

Those who insist history won't repeat itself point to the initial stages of the pandemic where, if anything, the financial markets benefited from central bank activities that were launched to ease the economic pain of the lockdowns. Confidence appeared high and remained so. At the same time, many (but by no means all) ordinary people have seen no real adverse economic impacts. The blow of unemployment was put off thanks to measures such as the furlough scheme and 'bounce back' loans for small businesses. A large proportion of the population even managed to *save* money during the various lockdowns.

But what these broad statements fail to address is what will happen when the globe tries to get back to normal and all the artificial stimuli are taken away. Once more, those who are convinced stagnation can't happen apparently have all the answers. One of the arguments frequently put across is that recovery may well be softer than expected and stretch out over a longer timescale, which means no alarming spikes. While yes, some people have saved money, there are millions of people worldwide who feel poorer as a result of the pandemic and so will be in no big rush to spend. Demand will be therefore be soft.

There is also a firm view that we won't see out-of-control pay rises as the recovery gets under way. For a classic wage spiral to develop and fuel inflation there would need to be two factors in play. In the first, employees would have to see their living standards eroded, which they have. However, for the second, they would need to be able to do something about it and the consensus is that today's workers hold a lot less power than their 1970s counterparts.

Fifty years ago, manufacturing accounted for a significantly larger chunk of the economy than it does now and trade union membership was high. Many industries were state-owned and trade had much more of a domestic focus, with far less competition from goods coming in from overseas. Widespread wage agreements guaranteed pay rises if inflation reached or passed certain levels. Therefore, workers of the 1970s were in a better position to do something about a squeeze on their incomes. We live and work in a very different world today. Prior to the pandemic, as many as 4.7 million workers – roughly one in ten working adults – worked in the gig economy in the UK.[10] Thanks to a boom in digital platforms such as Uber and Deliveroo, huge numbers have taken on casual and insecure platform work. Most are not protected by trades unions, so they don't have the strength in numbers of their 1970s forebears. Even if they did, there is little doubt that unions are in a far weaker bargaining position today, while employers have grown correspondingly stronger. Even in so-called traditional jobs, there is the threat that unemployment may keep on rising for some time to come, which limits the bargaining power of those with jobs when it comes to negotiating for higher pay.

Far from running out to the shops to splurge on goods to satisfy pent-up demand, households are more likely to be cautious, the anti-stagflation crowd will assure you. Many will have paid back their credit cards over lockdown, but while they have a little leeway, may be unwilling to return into debt. They are certainly unlikely to take out loans to fuel a spending spree, not at such an uncertain time. If this is the case, how else could a spending peak occur?

Each of these arguments has a counterargument. Right now, we have no way of really knowing how consumers will react post-pandemic and whether demand will soar, or show a more measured growth. While wages are likely to remain static, this is not the only inflationary force as I will now show. As for the reduced inclination in households to borrow, this counterargument may just be too linear. If individuals are less likely to take out loans, this, in turn, will reduce the amount of money in the system. Dig even further into this argument and a worrying picture emerges. Why do most consumers apply for loans? For the most part, it is so they can fund a large purchase, such as a house or a car. They certainly don't borrow a large amount of cash for their weekly shop, or a bit of a splurge at their favourite clothing chain. (It should be said, there are now specialist loan-service apps, such as Klarna and Affirm, that offer fast financing for online purchases, from clothing to furniture and electronics.) In the main, though, the prices of the basics at the supermarket will steadily rise, while the cost of homes, cars and other large assets begin to fall because there simply isn't the demand.

Uncertainty about the potential reaction of employers and consumers is not the only worrying trend. It is the reaction of the authorities, who will need to see off any threat of stagnation, that should be of greatest concern. Central bankers have long prided themselves on knowing which switches to throw to see off any threat of imbalance. Rising prices? Their monetary stance gets tightened via draconian interest-rate hikes. Rising employment? It's time to print more money to stimulate growth. But what weapons do these financial policy-makers have if both threats loom large *at the same time*? Answer: none. Simply putting more and more money into circulation will not solve the problem.

If stagflation does emerge, it will have a profound impact on all of us and the opportunities for individuals to keep their investments intact and their finances healthy will be vastly reduced. While the financial markets confounded expectations in 2020/21, we should all be thinking seriously about what happens after this period. If stagflation does loom, the investment climate will quickly begin to look quite different from anything seen in the last forty years. Stocks, bonds and commodities will start to move (downwards) in step and government or sovereign bonds in particular could take on a completely different character. In the 1970s, government bonds became almost as volatile as equities. In the worst years of stagflation, no asset classes at all produced positive real returns.[11]

The truth is, right now, there is little standing in the way of a period of Great Stagflation and simply denying it could happen will not ensure that we avoid it. While we remain in a situation where too few people feel prepared to admit the possibility of this phenomenon, let alone do anything about it, the onus is on individuals to do what they can to protect themselves and their finances. There are no 'solutions', but preparation is key.

# TWO

# A Perfect Storm

There was a long-running joke on Twitter throughout the first year of the COVID-19 pandemic. It was trotted out at each new unexpected and often bizarre development.

'Well, I didn't have that on my 2020 bingo card,' people would tweet.

Step away from the forest of shrugging emojis for a moment, though, and there is a serious point to be made here about the confluence of a series of events occurring around the pandemic, each of which adds fuel to the prospect of stagflation.

Throughout the pandemic individuals, quite naturally, looked to political leaders to act quickly and make decisions to bring about the best possible outcome socially and economically. Unfortunately, a hugely challenging situation has arguably been exacerbated by the political divides that were evident long before most people had even heard of COVID-19. In Europe, while parties of different persuasions were initially quite supportive of the lockdown restrictions that were imposed to stop the spread of the virus, the consensus was always quite fragile and quickly broke apart. Meanwhile, President Trump (who was already facing a gruelling re-election battle in the USA) found the disease taking centre-stage almost from day one of his campaign, fuelling the already acute hostility between Republicans and Democrats. Even the wearing of masks became politicised, with the decision whether or not to do so apparently being seen as a signal of an individual's allegiance. As the months wore on and people around the world grew tired of lockdown and increasingly concerned about the economic future, political divisions everywhere re-emerged with a vengeance. Politics seem to have become more polarised than ever with support for the far right and far left rising to dangerous levels across the globe.

There seems little to stop the worrying trend towards populism, nationalism and xenophobia that has thrived in the shadow of the pandemic. Certainly, some politicians are making no moves to curtail it. The Trump administration went to great lengths to blame China for the pandemic. Chinese President Xi Jinping responded by repeating his claim that the USA is doing its best to prevent China's peace and prosperity. These were not the only nations to go down this route (albeit they were the ones shouting the loudest in the first year of coronavirus). There have been widespread less-than-subtle hints of a backlash against democracy in response to the pandemic. Populist leaders the world over have benefited from economic weakness, mass unemployment and rising inequality. With heightened economic insecurity and no obvious quick fix, there has been an ever-stronger tendency to scapegoat foreigners and so win votes. The rhetoric is falling on willing ears too, with many voters (both skilled and unskilled workers) soaking up proposals to restrict migration and international trade. The move towards trade protection, accompanied by hostility towards former allies and trading partners, sets the stage for a new cold war. This time, technology is proving a powerful weapon in whipping up public support and we've seen growing evidence of clandestine cyber-warfare and interference in the electoral process of rival nations.

The fevered political landscape has made it almost impossible for governments to properly debate, let alone pass into law, the imaginative reforms that are so badly needed to reverse a substantial decline in economic and social circumstances. With their hands largely tied by a narrow populist agenda, which vastly reduces the options available, governments have in the main turned to the only (tried and tested) tool they currently have in their kitbag to stop deep and painful recessions: artificial stimulation of the economy. Printing money has only ever been a blunt tool at best, as we will see in more detail in Chapter Three, and it adds to the problem by driving up budget deficits. With no economic growth to help meet the deficit, successive governments will find themselves in a vicious circle: printing more money to solve the problem they created by printing money.

## The backlash against globalisation

It's not just restricted domestic policymaking that is troubling. The backlash against globalisation opposes a trade system that has been showing sustained and increasing growth since Japan adopted just-in-time production systems in the 1980s. The idea of low-cost global trade quickly caught on, fuelled by shrinking transportation costs, new technology and breakthroughs in supply chain logistics. Countries around the world benefited from this worldwide movement of goods. According to the International Monetary Fund (IMF), between 1993 and 2013 almost three-quarters of the increase in trade was attributable to growth in international supply chains.[12,13] During that twenty-year period, global trade rose five-fold. The most recent wave of trade openness flourished in the decade following 2001, when China became a member of the World Trade Organization. This marked a time when growth was strong, in part thanks to a globalisation virtuous circle, where cheaper imports pushed down inflation rates and allowed the West's central banks to keep interest rates and asset prices high.

Today, many nations are either talking about, or in the process of, bringing trade back home as part of a campaign to shield domestic firms and workers from global disruptions. This is not the first time we have experienced deglobalisation. Although international supply chains were markedly less sophisticated in the twentieth century, there was a period of domestic retrenchment during the tough years between 1914 and 1945. Now though, deglobalisation is happening to a far, far greater extent due to geopolitics, struggling domestic economies and rising fiscal inequality. Countries get defensive when times are tough and things have not been this tough for generations.

Analysts and commentators are already saying that the era of open markets and open borders, where trade and capital flows freely around the world, has run its course. Everywhere you look, there are examples of countries retrenching. In the UK, efforts that began before the pandemic to beef up UK supply chains and encourage manufacturers to favour domestic production have gathered momentum. (This was also prompted by Brexit.) Nearly two-thirds of UK manufacturers believe the health crisis has triggered widespread 'reshoring' strategies.[14] In the USA, throughout his term President Trump talked about bringing trade back from China, introduced punitive tariffs on imports from China and anti-China measures for American companies. The stance was initially triggered by perception that the rise of China was a strategic threat to American dominance in trade, and the health emergency gave the protectionist president even more ammunition. It is too early to say how much of this shift President Joe Biden will seek to reverse and, if so, how far. Deglobalisation is a trend that is being repeated throughout the world. The World Trade Organization forecast that global trade would decline by between 13% and 32% in 2020, which was much more than the expected fall in gross domestic product (GDP).[15] Few political leaders have rushed to contradict this assumption. French President Emmanuel Macron said COVID would 'change the nature of globalisation, with which we have lived for the past forty years' and that it was 'clear that this kind of globalisation was reaching the end of its cycle'.[16] For other nations, actions have spoken louder than words. A large, ¥243 billion chunk of Japan's economic support package has been earmarked to help manufacturers shift production out of China after the pandemic disrupted supply chains between these major trading partners.[17] With the frailties of the global supply chains exposed, the momentum towards reshoring is only going to increase. The post-pandemic world will be marked by tighter restrictions on the movement of goods, services, capital, labour, technology, data and information.

The trend away from globalisation might have arisen without the impetus provided by the pandemic. The financial crisis of 2008/9 exposed many of the weaknesses of a global system that operates without adequate controls or any sort of effective supervision. The resulting slump is etched deep in our collective memories, which is why many countries have already erred on the side of caution. There has also been an awakening, albeit slow, to the fact that the fruits of globalisation are primarily, although not exclusively, enjoyed by the owners of capital and global elites. We've all benefited from lower prices, but there is no escaping the growth in inequality between the haves and the have nots. The stagnation, or slow growth, in general living standards is what, in great part, has already been responsible for fuelling nationalism. Pre-pandemic, there were noises about some sort of internationally coordinated move to match politics to economics and organise capital on a global level, followed by some sort of across-the-board democratic mechanism, but the chances of that happening now are less than zero. With the added impetus of the pandemic, the move away from globalisation is all but assured.

Does it matter? Well, yes. While the rush to protect supplies is understandable, there are several very large flaws in the anti-globalisation strategy, particularly in relation to looming stagflation. Switching location to domestic production means prices will need to go up because we don't have legions of cheap workers in the West. In countries with a minimum wage, workers need to be paid much more than their counterparts in countries like Bangladesh. They need to be given better working conditions too. Another consequence of widespread reshoring is that more money will stay in the country. When we buy goods from abroad, currency flows out of the country to pay for the products which flow in. If we buy goods made here, more currency remains in the domestic market. However, this should alarm everyone because this money will now be sloshing around alongside all that virtual QE cash. This, in turn, stimulates domestic consumer price inflation because the money supply is *higher* but the price of goods has probably had to rise (those expensive local workers), which proba-bly means the supply of goods is *lower*. As well as the need to pay domestic workers more and the increase in the domestic cash pile, there is also the potential for a triple whammy: China might react quite badly to Western businesses' decision to reshore. It seems likely, on past form, that China will weaponise its supply chains in retaliation, causing bottlenecks in the goods that it does supply (China is a major global component supplier: the bits manufacturers need to build things with), further destabilis-ing an already fragile system. A new world of fragmented, unstable supply chains could well provoke panic-buying and further fuel inflation.

## Have we been here before?

If you are the type who likes to play the sleuth and check the veracity of these arguments (and please do), some valuable clues from the history books might cast light on our current situa-tion. One of the factors blamed for worsening the Great Depression of almost a century ago was the Smoot-Hawley Tariff Act of 1930. In a bid to support US farmers who were suffering, the legislation raised tariffs on thousands of imported goods by an average of 40% to 50%. Tariffs are, of course, nothing more than a tax on the movement of goods from one country to another. They create what is known as a 'dead-weight loss', distorting supply and demand dynamics. Often, the outcome of higher tariffs is that prices to consumers rise at the same time as producers see their margins compressed and orders decline in volume. This is exactly what happened following the Smoot-Hawley intervention. Other countries retaliated with their own tariffs, forcing global trade down by 65%, while food prices in the USA rose. It was a disaster by any measure, achieving little but uniting most economists to regard this sort of trade protectionism as dangerous.

It would be odd to assume that things would be different this time around. Globalism is not a tap that is easily turned off. Perhaps just as importantly, these supply chains have been recognised as a crucial source of *dis*inflation. Before the pandemic, it was estimated that global inflation would have been 1% higher, if it were not for the efficiencies of the international supply chains.[18] The proportion of goods that are imported and exported is far greater today than a century ago. There is also more money and credit in circulation. With savings rates broadly unchanged after factoring in the increase in consumer debt, monetary expansion fuels price inflation and a trade deficit. When consumers buy cheaper foreign goods, the trade deficit can help to defer price inflation. Take away that option by raising trade tariffs and everyone will be faced with rising prices. Without a compensating increase in wages, either consumers will need to take on more credit (and in Chapter One I pointed out that they don't seem to be doing that) or they will simply buy less, which will depress demand and undermine domestic output. Factory activity will plummet. There is, after all, no point in making goods no one can afford (or is prepared) to buy. The contraction in global trade will make inflation more likely and take a huge chunk out of domestic economies, adding to the prospect of unemployment. Did you have that on your 2020 bingo card?

The switch away from globalisation is not the only red flashing light we should be thinking about right now. We are in a very different world from even a few decades ago, when reshoring might have meant opening up factories and ramping up production of physical goods. Future growth will almost inevitably come from tech and, even before the pandemic, we saw even traditional industries moving towards digitalisation. This doesn't just spell a big change in the way we produce goods, it also means that now we only need a far smaller and more skilled workforce. While digital technology will play a big part in fuelling the post-coronavirus recovery, the economy will rely on different talents and many fewer workers. Large numbers of employers will have no need to re-engage unskilled workers, many of whom were furloughed at the beginning of the pandemic, leading to a large wave of redundancies. The further downward pressure on jobs and wages thanks to automation will fan the flames of populism, nationalism and xenophobia.

The digital trend opens up another worrying component in our perfect storm: a reduction in opportunities for the younger generation, which will have an impact on the wider economy. While it is often said that youngsters today were practically born with a smartphone in their hands and are really tech-savvy, this is not universally true. In the UK, the educational sector has long been in dire need of realignment with the economy and many state institutions have missed the boat on tech. As a result of widespread cut-backs in school budgets, many youngsters have had little or no access to digital skills training, despite there being a very clear need for it. The OBR is already forecasting that an additional 600,000 18–24-year-olds will be pushed into unemployment in the first year after lockdown measures end,[19] but if they do not have the skills to take up digital jobs, there is even less opportunity for them to fight their way into the workplace.

What happens to our young people is concerning by any measure, but what makes it a particular issue is another element in our perfect storm: the demographic time bomb. The West is faced with a rapidly ageing population as its collective age rises at an unprecedented pace.

Thanks to advances in healthcare that have greatly contributed to longevity, a 100-year lifespan is much less unlikely than it used to be. In 2019, over 31% of the UK population were aged 55 or above.[20] Nine out of the ten largest economies in the world, which represent a combined 88.5% of global GDP, face this threat. (India is the only outlier – representing 3% of global GDP.) Even before COVID-19, this was recognised as a looming crisis. With more individuals reaching the age at which they could retire, there are implications for healthcare provision, pension rates and taxes, all of which may have to push costs up or else put a further strain on public coffers and economic growth. If the next generation in line, and the next, are not in work to pay these taxes, where does the money come from?

The pandemic exacerbated the trend, straining health and social care systems, and provides a very real demonstration of how hard-pressed and under-resourced these public services are. It also knocked retirement planning sideways for many people, with uncertain investment markets, interest rates at rock bottom and large businesses pulling back on dividend payments, which is something that many pension plans rely on.

It doesn't help that pension planning and provision never really recovered properly from the 2008/9 crisis. Back then, one in ten organisations put a hold on matching pension contributions as they struggled to stay afloat, permanently putting a dent into the finances and long-term plans of many households. Since then, some countries, including the UK and the USA, introduced measures to allow people to take their pensions early. In the UK, for example, anyone over the age of 55 can take their whole pension savings as a lump sum, paying no tax on the first 25%. The move to introduce this 'freedom' flew in the face of arguments that this was saving up an even bigger headache for later on. Some estimates have claimed that up to 50% of the older generation may have to delay retirement, or live off a vastly reduced sum, because of over-ambitious investment withdrawals and reduced contributions.[21] What this all means is that many more pensioners will have to turn to some form of state aid. Once again: where will all this money come from?

It is inevitable that funding these pension/savings deficits will make the debts from today's under-funded healthcare and social security systems even larger. Moving forward, there will be less money to pass on to children and, as life expectancy increases, children will be far older when they inherit from their parents, if they inherit at all. With governments needing to take up the slack, spending more on pensions and healthcare will crowd out money for any other potential approaches to the problem of stagflation. There will be less money going into savings and capital investment.

The final point to be made about the conditions that have created our perfect stagflation storm is that we should have started battening down the hatches and preparing for it a long time ago. Just as successive governments had drawn up pandemic plans and then seemingly shelved them just when they might have come in handy, the authorities had an inkling that we were heading into an uncertain financial future, but powered ahead anyhow. Much of what we are experiencing now has been exacerbated by policy mistakes made following the 2008/9 global economic crisis. In the rush to get things 'back to normal', little thought was given to addressing the structural problems that led to the worldwide financial collapse in the first place. Far from going away, the problems with the world economy have actually grown since the era of the Global Credit Crunch, making us vulnerable to a deeper recession in future, with wider-reaching consequences than past ones. All that was required was a trigger to set it off. A trigger like, say, a global health crisis.

To make matters worse, we are less well-equipped today to deal with the ramifications of an economic crisis. In 2008, when the news broke about the dire situation that many banks had fallen into, interest rates were high enough to give central banks at least a little wriggle room when it came to alleviating the fall-out. This option is no longer available today, with interest rates at rock bottom. Government debt in most economies in 2008 was also significantly below danger levels. That is not the case today, after extensive periods of QE in the interim; now we are staring at a sovereign debt mountain. It's hardly a great point to start looking for urgent solutions to a significant economic crisis.

Everywhere you look, there are signs that no one is prepared for what is to come. The banks that were so central to the last crisis have yet to fully repair their balance sheets. Even the countries that successfully navigated 2008/9 are in a weakened position. The Asian markets, and in particular China, which barely wobbled during the Global Credit Crunch, were previously viewed as the drivers of the next wave. Yet, even prior to COVID-19, there were already signs this was not as firm a bet as it might be. China was dealing with a property bubble and inflation, twin factors that caused the government to rein in the economy. Then, of course, the coronavirus hit and China, like everywhere else in the world, has had to deal with it. There is little point, either, in looking to individual households to hold their own as things begin to get tough. The years since 2008 have seen rising levels of personal debt versus low confidence, particularly in countries that have followed austerity policies. Meanwhile, even before the pandemic, employment prospects were not encouraging as firms increasingly embraced the gig economy, putting workers on uncertain short-term contracts.

We are, without a doubt, facing a day of reckoning. In the boom times, governments around the world pushed the boundaries, with deregulation, privatisation and free-trade policies. In a world where everyone seemed to be prospering, countries in the West were happy to export jobs to lower-wage countries. The pay-off seemed certain: costs and domestic inflation would fall because jobs, mainly in the service sector, were being created. Times have now changed. A lot. In the aftermath of COVID-19, we are facing lower growth rates, a complete rebalancing of global trade and increased protectionism. There is no doubt that the recession will accelerate the reshaping of many industries, with a vastly increased reliance on technology. Many more businesses will fail and mature businesses will be under pressure to consolidate, or sell off unprofitable parts. Meanwhile, we will experience the twin pressures of rising unemployment, particularly among the young, and increasing numbers retiring. After failing to properly deal with the aftermath of the Global Credit Crunch, governments are even less prepared to deal with the looming crisis and have a limited number of options. With so many negative factors converging at once, this is not the sort of economic event that we can spend our way out of. Yet, as we will see in Chapter Three, right now that is precisely Plan A.

# THREE

# The Flawed Response

During the first nine months of the pandemic, the Bank of England pumped an additional £450 billion into the economy via a QE programme of bond-buying in a bid to ease what is expected to be the worst recession in living memory thanks to a record collapse in output.[22] This, it was said at the time, was one of the few options open to the central bank. The other option, cutting interest rates, which is the usual first response when economic times are hard, was a non-starter: interest rates had already been cut to just above zero. While there was a brief period of speculation that the Bank of England could have opted for negative rates as a tool to bolster activity, this idea was dismissed. Thus, it was decided that the only way to encourage spending and investment was to inject more money into circulation.

This was not, as the saying goes, the Bank of England's first rodeo. It launched its first QE programme in 2009, when the meltdown in the global financial markets threatened the economy and stock markets were in free fall. The idea behind QE is that a central bank creates virtual money to buy corporate and government bonds from banks. The knock-on effect is that interest rates fall, borrowing increases and consumers go out and spend more. This helps businesses and revives the economy. *Voilà*! The initial credit crunch programme that issued £75 billion in November 2009 quickly ballooned to £200 billion when the economy took longer than hoped to show signs of recovery. Then, in 2012, when the eurozone debt crisis hit, the Bank of England kicked out a further £175 billion. Four years later, a further £75 billion in QE rolled out of the Bank, in response to the Brexit referendum result.[23] At the time of writing, if you include the billions injected during 2020, the QE programme totals £875 billion.

There can be no doubt that, despite the fact it was initially billed as a temporary, emergency measure, QE has become the go-to strategy of central banks despite the fact history is rich with examples of the strategy of expanding base money as an added stimulant to encourage growth coming unstuck. The first time it happened in modern times was following the postwar slump in 1920–21. The US Federal Reserve Bank (Fed), which came into being before the First World War, presided over a monetary expansion, which as we all now know led to the Wall Street Crash, the results of which reverberated throughout the world. Oddly, instead of going back to the drawing board and thinking *hey, that didn't work out well, did it?* central bankers doubled down on the policy, injecting even more cash into the system. The process set in train a series of business cycles and market fluctuations, some minor and some significant, but each with important knock-on consequences. Take the monetary expansion of the early 1970s as a case in point. You will recall that this is the decade where we saw stagflation for the first time. When coupled with the abandonment of the gold standard in 1971, a US QE policy helped fuel price inflation throughout the decade. Inflation drove oil and energy prices upwards, handing more power to OPEC. It also undermined the purchasing power of several countries' currencies, making the interest rate rises of the early 1980s inevitable. Amazingly, even then lessons were not learned. Central banks not only ploughed on with injecting virtual cash into circulation, they actually accelerated QE. Just to add volatility to the mix, there were a number of reforms of the financial system in the 1980s, such as the integration of bank investment and retail operations, expanding bank credit into market-making, proprietary trading and derivatives. The result? No less than three inflationary peaks in securities markets in relatively quick succession: the dot-com boom, the residential property and stock market booms of the early 2000s and the boom which rapidly followed the 2008/09 financial crash.

Each of these mini-, or maxi-, booms have been the result of a series of man-made, monetary inflations targeted at financial asset prices. Every time, the booms have little to do with reality on the ground. Indeed, the growth in the productive side of Western economies has mainly been stagnant (even before COVID-19) and has largely been kept afloat by the expansion of consumer credit. Perhaps most crucially, the rapid succession of credit cycles, with each folding into the next, means there is never any true recovery. Malinvestments are not unwound, or adjusted, they are simply swallowed up by the next boom. If you add it all together, though, it adds up to a far greater elevation of credit than the one that caused the greatest depression of modern times in the 1920/30s.

## QE: should we worry?

This is not the only reason we should be concerned about QE as the go-to 'solution' to this, or any other financial crisis. While we have grown used to the ebb and flow of the money cycle and the periodic crises which turn out to be either bumps in the road or full-blown bank crises, like the one we saw in 2008/9, what should be concerning us is the many City and Wall Street strategists, market-makers and investors that have learned to use the central bank countermeasures to their advantage. We've seen increasing examples of these fiscal measures being used as the foundation for ever-more risky behaviour and dubious investments, rather than strategies that make sense on a sound commercial basis. These questionable practices are enabled by the system of fractional reserve banking, the most common form of banking practised by commercial banks, which means making loans to borrowers while holding in reserve only a fraction of what the bank owes to its deposit investors. The increase in bank credit fuels risky and opportunistic investment strategies. Thus, the greater the expansion of credit, the greater the risk of an eventual crash and the greater the size of that crash. The QE strategy being pursued by central banks is actually storing up problems for the future.

Monetarist theory explains this neatly with the simple formula MV = PQ, where M is the money supply, V is the velocity or number of times in a year it is spent, P is the price of goods and services, and Q is the quantity of goods and services. If a nation's supply of money increases, economic activity will increase, and the reverse is also true. If M is increased, either P, Q or both P and Q rise. If manufacturers can charge more and sell at the higher prices so Q does not fall, fine; if they have to raise prices and cut production (Q) to compensate, less good; but if they can't balance P and Q, V will fall: people and businesses stop buying goods and services. Added to this, in a difficult long-term slump, people will use their money to pay off debts, rather than investing in (costly) goods and services.

Many respected economists have long argued that QE doesn't work. Professor William Perraudin, an economist at Imperial College London, said that the idea that it has any 'significant impact on real activity is pretty dubious', while Richard Murphy, an economist and accountant who runs Tax Research UK, said that it will 'improve banks' liquidity, not the UK economy'.[24] Another way to put this is: it's made the super-rich richer, but done very little for the rest of society and has, in fact, adversely impacted the vast majority in a big way.

The phenomenon of stagflation puts even more pressure on the already flawed strategy of QE. We can't simply ride out stagflation in the same way as we have the other crises. Nor can we keep issuing virtual money indefinitely, especially if stagflation looms. Stagflation creates a highly dynamic situation which will thwart policymakers in their bids to stabilise things. Let me explain why.

While visiting the Magic Money Tree as a primary response to the pandemic might seem prudent, that policy is even less appropriate under this specific set of circumstances. To begin with, it entails a massive increase in fiscal deficits (ie tax revenue failing to cover government spending). This is worrying because of both past and future influences. Governments are still carrying high debts racked up in the 'recovery' from the last big slump. Moving forward, many households and businesses have lost income, which means private sector debt levels will soar, with the potential for mass default and bankruptcies in the months and years ahead. Meanwhile, more public spending needs to be allocated to healthcare, not just because of the pandemic and its after-effects, but because of the demographic time bomb thanks to an ageing population. That's not to forget an increasing pension burden with so many older people retiring early, either because they want to, or have to.

Let's play out the scenario of the large increase in money in circulation, to see its logical conclusion. To simplify matters hugely, imagine the additional cash that central banks are happily issuing goes straight into our pockets. *There you go, it's been a tough few years, you deserve it.* As we know, the idea is that we'll go out and spend this money, thus oiling the wheels of the economy and getting everything moving again. Unfortunately, following the pandemic, our spending options have vastly reduced. That nice restaurant we used to visit with our family has closed its doors permanently; it was unable to survive the extended lockdowns. The same goes for that friendly local shop we always liked to visit in a bid to support our community. In fact, there will be substantially fewer places to buy the goods we need now. What happens when the supply options decrease at the same time as the amount of money in circulation increases? When goods are scarce, sellers can put their prices up and we have price inflation. It's a seller's market – for those sellers that are still trading.

There are many other reasons why the QE policy will quickly unravel. Right now, the relative stability of the financial markets is based on the widely held assumption that central banks around the globe can pull off their usual magic and calm everything down, bring it into line. In the past, for example, if central banks wanted credit spreads to come down to a certain level, they made more money available so banks would have to cut their charges in order to sell loans. Likewise with mortgage spreads and so on. If any central bank says they want the three-year interest rate to be a certain percentage, they could play with supply and demand to get what they want. If the economy starts to stagnate, freedom to do this is severely constrained, thanks to inflation and the resulting strain on currency. If policymakers are proved to be powerless to achieve their goals, however much tinkering they do (and a major goal will be to bring unemployment rates down significantly), that's going to be a big issue. The market-makers will wake up to the somewhat startling and unsettling possibility that neither they nor the authorities can control market sentiment: how much people want to go to market. The certainty and predictability of the mini- and maxi-booms will be over.

At some point the penny will drop and the realisation will dawn: we face a choice between inflation and 'acceptable' unemployment rates. How individual countries choose to go from there will be up to each jurisdiction. Uncertainty will reign supreme as different policymakers across the globe plot their paths through these difficult conditions. (And we all know how the markets hate uncertainty.) Some big decisions will need to be made. What, for example, would a country do if faced with a 10% unemployment rate and inflation hits 4% or 5%? Just as we saw in the 1970s, there will be a trade-off between quite weak economic conditions and higher inflation, on one hand, and raising real rates to offset these, on the other. It was a very problematic policy position then and it won't be any easier today. Don't forget, there is already a deep current of public unrest and there have been a number of well-attended demonstrations against government policies. It wouldn't take much for things to spill over into a very volatile situation indeed, further adding to the problem.

There is no doubt at all that the post-coronavirus economic problem we face is much larger than it has been painted, even though most rational observers would accept that times will be tough when the day of reckoning comes. Our inability to see things for what they are is perhaps exacerbated by the fact we tend to paint all economic problems with the same broad brush. *Downturns are painful, but we seem to get through them in a few years. Boom times always come back quite quickly.* We defer to experts, even though they have only mapped out their macro-understanding of what a slowdown means to corporate balance sheets at one moment in time. The difference today is that, following the prolonged effects of the pandemic, we are still only seeing part of the picture. Early estimates show that the first wave of the pandemic and measures to slow its spread cost the global economy $3.8 trillion and put 147 million people out of work.[25] Global wages dropped by $2.1 trillion, or about 6% of worldwide income. The reduction in international trade left a $536 billion black hole.[26] This though, as we now know, was just the start. The shocks to the labour market grew as the multi-million-dollar rescue and support packages brought in by successive governments were eased. It was always inevitable that companies seeking to shore up their finances would embark on large-scale redundancies and cut back on their spending, with the knock-on effect that suppliers have had to cut their costs further too. As predicted, we are already seeing fewer significant asset purchases, or indeed mergers and acquisitions (M&A) activity. To date, the negative impact of this 'second stage' in the slowdown has yet to be fully built into official estimates.

Ah, you may say, we can just go on printing more money until there is a correction. But central banks can't go on issuing money indefinitely while buying assets to support markets. Any wealth, whether it is a debt someone owes you or an imbalance in an equity valuation, is a draw on somebody's future income. Someone has to pay back that debt or, if you are a shareholder, generate profits out of which to pay dividends to you. If everything is too far out of whack, incomes can't cover these liabilities and wealth will fall to reflect that. Central banks can't change the physics of that basic truth. The only tool they really have at their disposal is to drive asset prices up so asset valuations appear able to support the promises the government, company or individual has made. This means the banks must go on issuing money, to create the inflation that keeps asset valuations high. Without this, either incomes or asset values will have to fall; or both. Eventually though, it is inevitable that we will have to reconcile assets with earnings. This will be either through convergence – financial markets falling so asset valuations appear in line with future commitments – or via inflation, driving up incomes and asset prices in step. One of these things has to happen to reconcile wealth (asset valuations) with income (individual earnings, company revenues, government tax receipts).

There are other reasons, too, why the central bank response this time needs to be different. Downturns are typically caused by too much credit. Indeed, most of the recessions over the last fifty years have been characterised by central banks tightening to try to head off inflation. They respond by raising interest rates, to cut off credit, which leads to a weakening in income. We face a very different set of circumstances today. It is the direct fall in income that has kicked it all off. Indeed, in 2020 we may well have seen the (unwanted) record for the fastest collapse of income and spending that most of us have experienced in living memory. The knock-on effect of a drop in income is a downward spiral. If one person's income falls, they stop spending, which in turn impacts other people's income. The collapse in spending almost immediately leads to a wider collapse in demand. This scenario presents a challenge to policymakers. It is a completely different kind of challenge, working out a strategy to shore up income, than dealing with credit. Issuing more money may have seemed to fix credit shortages, but the same strategy is not as effective at fixing an income shortfall. How can printing money make up for the loss in income of, say, a pub worker who is now out of a job? This person's situation, and that of millions like them, is much less directly connected to the financial markets, so less easy to solve with the one-size-fits-all mallet of QE.

## The almighty dollar

The response, or lack of response, of one nation in particular, the USA, has also raised concerns. Thanks to the Trump administration's lack of response to COVID-19, it has now been openly suggested that the dollar might lose its hallowed place as the reserve currency. This status has long held several benefits to its host country, such as unrivalled demand from investors world-wide to own dollar-denominated assets such as Treasury bonds, which in turn allows the USA to borrow at lower rates than might otherwise have been the case. Also, the bulk of global financial markets are priced in dollars, including commodities such as oil, gold, base metals and agricultural products, which protects the USA from exchange rate risks. However, it has done few other nations any favours. It wasn't just America's failure to get to grips with the pandemic that rattled markets around the world, it was also the country's long-term persistence in using QE and ultra-low interest rates, and a concerted drive to encourage higher inflation.

The USA had been thought less vulnerable to a crisis like the one we are seeing today because the dollar's reserve currency status meant such vast international investments in the dollar that a downturn could probably be absorbed without a significant problem. However, if reserve currency status is under stress, and if the dollar might lose that status, the USA may lose the ability to manage its economy as it has done. This risks becoming a self-fulfilling prophecy, where spiralling inflation jeopardises reserve currency status, making the dollar more inflationary and reducing the chances their economy might recover.

The vulnerability of the dollar is not just bad news for the USA. While a change to the status quo might be advantageous in the long run, the dollar is still at the centre of all of our economies today, which exposes everyone to risk. If we continue on the current trajectory, we may face a disorderly and rapid devaluation of the dollar which will spook the entire investment community. This could lead to a rapid sell-off of US bonds, which will quickly escalate as other investors spot the trend. Interest rates would shoot upwards as investors around the world try to liquidate their positions, sending the dollar even lower. Anyone who reacted too slowly would be left holding a huge number of plummeting dollars. Every country in the world would see catastrophic losses, on top of the peril in which COVID-19 has already placed them. It is conceivable that a cascading wave of defaults would push the entire global financial system into collapse.

Despite all the warning signs outlined here, there are no clear signs that central banks are even contemplating a change of approach. There is little point looking to individual governments to step in and be the voice of reason, either. As previously noted, politics the world over is acutely polarised, with governments drifting towards extreme positions, right and left, rather than working to improve the lot of the majority in the middle. Despite signs of growing social unrest, fuelled by the varying and at times erratic political response to the pandemic, there is little hope that things will stabilise once the crisis is past. In the ensuing volatile environment, it will be very difficult to pass meaningful reforms, or write new legislation, even if there was the political will to do so. We are at a crucial moment in history. We need to find a way to adapt to the new economic and social landscape, and ensure either that stagflation is avoided, or that the pain it causes does not endure. Without a coherent policy, central banks may believe the only course of action that appears available will be to keep on stimulating the economy artificially, despite the fact that this is only making the situation worse.

# FOUR

# Just How Bad Could It Get?

No one can fail to be aware that the economic fall-out from COVID-19 will be severe. Just how severe and when it will truly impact remains to be seen. Since the first news of the pandemic broke and casualties began to emerge around the world, economic conditions have been closely tied to the virus's trajectory. The decline in output and employment levels quickly exceeded those of the 2008/9 crisis and occurred much more rapidly. While there was early, hopeful, talk of a V-shaped recovery, as the first wave flowed into the second, and then the third, analysts acknowledged that getting back on top of things may take longer than first hoped.

When it comes to stagflation, the big question is: if an individual does not immediately lose their job, or find their business failing, when will they feel the impact? Strangely, the ordinary person on the street may not be aware of the economic shift straight away, which may serve initially to mask just how bad things are going to get. The prices of goods and services, as measured by the Consumer Price Index (CPI), may well remain steady for a good while. This is thanks in great part to the growth in the use of technology. It has been said that the uptake of digital moved forward twenty years or more in the space of a year during 2020, as individuals and organisations raced to find new ways of doing things in vastly changed circumstances. You'll understand the phenomenon if you were previously a technophobe; even if you were competent with a computer, you'll know people who once weren't. When the first lockdown struck, people raced to learn how to use Zoom,

Slack and many other means of communication that would keep them connected with their work and their loved ones. Multiply this new reality many times to understand how businesses far and wide raced to adopt tech to keep the lights on and money coming in. For everyone the result has been the same: there will be no going back. Digital has opened up a new world, where it is faster, cheaper and more convenient to let the computers do the work. The broader digital disruption of the economy will initially act as a powerful deflationary force, pushing down the cost of consumer goods and services. Outdated versions of goods will be replaced with cheaper, more efficient alternatives. As already noted, over time this digitalisation will have more ominous implications for stagnation. With many nations choosing to reshore, any factories that have not already done so will be redesigned to use as few human workers as possible. Production will increase, but employment might not; it might even fall. In the early days, though, digital will be a life-saver, keeping inflation low and the wheels turning.

The only hint of what is to come is in the rising prices for stocks and property. Indeed, the early days of the pandemic witnessed a mini-boom in house sales thanks to the large number of now-homeworkers relocating from cities to seek more affordable, yet spacious, country homes. Elsewhere, it took time for business to change and the financial markets gave us few clues about what was to come. Even in the worst days of the first and second waves of the pandemic, the S&P 500 in the USA only slipped a few percentage points below where it started the year and at many moments was *ahead* of its level a year before.[27] In the UK, the FTSE remained fairly solid, despite the very clear red flag raised by the OECD, which predicted the country was likely to suffer more than any country in the developed world.[28]

The clear implication of this market resilience was that the majority of investors believed that things would bounce back to normal swiftly. The thinking seemed to go that a vaccine would be found and quickly rolled out, the authorities would take control and any setbacks would only be temporary. The general mood seemed to be one of confidence, anticipating that any rise in unemployment would be successfully reversed and once people were earning again and the shops were open, demand would rapidly rise back to pre-coronavirus levels. This confidence was helped along by regular pronouncements from the Bank of England and the US Fed that they would pretty much issue all the money needed to support the economy and keep asset prices up. This approach was repeated across the globe, with the European Central Bank (ECB) embarking on a €600 billion round of bond buying and the Japanese government pledging a stimulus package equivalent to 40% of GDP. In short, a veritable wall of money entered the system, which helped keep the markets calm.

## Language matters

Aside from the reasons why QE is not a 'solution' (see Chapter Three), other factors underline the entirely false assumptions that the markets have been operating under. These, in turn, mean their response to the situation is misguided, since it is based upon a misleading impression that everything is a lot better than it actually is, which is clearly a dangerous and unsustainable position. What could lie at the heart of the problem is the language used to describe what might come next. Whenever the prospect of a pandemic-induced downturn is raised, it is always discussed in the terms used to describe a 1930s-style deflationary depression. This is perhaps because the media like a dramatic hook to hang a story on, so it is an easy shorthand to refer to the Great Recession, or the Great Depression, to get across that things are very grave indeed. In fact, this moniker is quite misleading. Yes, the downturn will be severe, but we will be in territory very different from the Depression of just over a century ago because we will be in the midst of an *inflationary* depression. With government spending propping up demand, even as unemployment soars, the inflation that is the inevitable result of this strategy will lead to a prolonged period of stagflation.

It is this nuance in language, deflationary versus inflationary, that appears to be confusing the financial markets and leading to the strange anomaly of the markets continuing at all-time-high levels, just before things are about to get very tough indeed. (And that's an understatement.) Those schooled in macroeconomics tend to have a black and white view of how things work. Inflation is viewed as a stimulant, while deflation causes depressions. But an economic depression is not simply a contraction of money in circulation, it is the collective impoverishment of a nation, which is most easily achieved by debasing the currency: monetary inflation. Yet central bankers, government economists and the private sector continue to prop up the myth that inflating the money supply is the key to economic recovery. Keep issuing money and the worst that can happen will be a mild recession before economic growth resumes, they say. As a result, save for a few lone voices warning of imminent meltdown, the world of investment remains as bullish as ever and no one acknowledges what is around the corner.

Why does this matter? Well, the slow response of the markets will play its part in delaying any meaningful and impactful response to the problem. If everything seems to be bumping along OK and the financial markets remain buoyant, there is no impetus to change tack, pause for a moment and consider that flooding the market with cash is perhaps not the best solution. The worry is that when inflation does noticeably rise, it may be assumed that this rise is cost-push inflation, prices rising due to higher production or raw material costs. This is the cyclical inflation we are all familiar with, and is relatively easy to deal with, by slowing down the economy to bring it in line. Monetary inflation is entirely different because, before anything can be manoeuvred into line, a budget deficit must be filled while income is lacking. That's not easy and there is no quick fix, particularly if central banks are starting from entirely the wrong place by churning out money.

Once again, let's play this out. How bad could it get? If, say, inflation passed 10% on the goods and services we buy every day and unemployment stood at 15% or higher, it's easy to see we would have reached a very bad position. However, it is useful to look at previous downturns to understand just how bad things can get. One useful, albeit basic, measure is the 'Misery Index', an economic indicator created by economist Arthur Okun to determine how the average citizen is doing economically, which is calculated by adding the unemployment rate to the annual inflation rate. Okun's original US-centred model was subsequently built upon by Johns Hopkins University economist Steve Hanke, who applied it to other countries. The modified index is the sum of:

interest rate + inflation rate + unemployment rate – year-over-year percentage change in per capita GDP growth.

As you might expect, the Misery Index was very high in the 1970s, peaking at 31% in 1975. While the Index entered the 1980s at a worrying 28%,[29] it fell steeply under Margaret Thatcher's policy to tame inflation through steep rises in the Bank of England's base rate and measures to slash employment, dropping to 13% by 1988. The Misery Index mostly remained low in the 1990s, falling to 7% in the quarter before the millennium. Then, after a relatively quiet beginning to the new century, it soared to 11% in 2008 as the Global Credit Crunch began to bite. If we took the original Okun calculation, the Misery Index could rise to 25% in the coming months. It could, quite possibly, be far higher.

So far, not so good. But there is more. It is widely acknowledged that there can be no sustainable recovery until the virus is *fully* contained. While this eventuality is helped by vaccines, a vaccine can never be a miracle cure and send everything back to normal. Moreover, a vaccine can only work properly if most people around the world get one. The virus spreads quickly and it can mutate: new strains have already appeared in England, South Africa, Brazil and no doubt elsewhere. This factor alone casts doubt on the general assumption that the more affluent economies will weather the crisis better than the ones that cannot afford rapid mass vaccination programmes. We really are all in this together. This presents the problem of as many people as possible being given the vaccine at broadly the same time. Many who are offered it won't take it, thanks to the burgeoning anti-vax campaign. If there is a recovery, it is likely to come in fits and starts. It is also likely to take far, far longer than most people expect. The recovery will also be a lot slower than those following previous slowdowns, because COVID-19 is probably, like flu, going to be with us for the rest of our lives.

# The 'new normal'

Most people are thoroughly sick of this phrase, but the changes to how we all now live will play their part in how we recover and how quickly. The changes to the job market have been substantial and permanent. There has been a huge reduction in the numbers of small businesses as many that managed to stumble through the early months of the pandemic were forced to close their doors despite the government bail-outs. Big businesses, while adversely impacted, have survived better than their smaller counterparts. These organisations now call the shots when it comes to hiring workers and it is fairly certain there will be a steady shift towards hiring gig workers, contractors and freelancers; we've already seen the first signs of it. The wider jobs market will be increasingly characterised by substantial cuts and many full-time positions may become part-time or temporary. Meanwhile, homeworking has become the norm for many, accelerating the decline of many city-centre jobs in the service industries that once relied upon commuters. We can also expect increased concentration and decreased competition in some sectors.

The pandemic-induced slowdown is, of course, global. In a fully synchronised crisis like this, there are fewer opportunities to address domestic impacts, or tighten national credit markets. Social safety nets are under more pressure than in living memory. Healthcare systems, even in well-off countries, are buckling under the strain. There will be a huge human cost, as many families struggle to buy food. We've already seen a surge in use of food banks. Governments struggling to cope with the human toll will default on debt. They are likely to fall back even harder on protectionist policies, which in turn will permanently change the competitiveness of many nations and their standing in the world. The crisis in international trade will undermine the creditworthiness of domestic businesses.

It is inevitable that there will eventually be a tipping point in the financial markets. Strong bullish forces – low interest rates and issuing money – will collide head-on with strong bearish forces – low economic growth, high unemployment and deficits. This is the point at which there will be very high stock market volatility. Take Treasury bonds as an example, to see what may happen. Say inflation rose from just 1% to 4%, even though this is a very conservative estimate. Ten-year Treasury bonds, which have interest rates close to zero today, would need an inflation premium. The markets cried foul when central banks tried to raise rates above 2% a few years back. They just couldn't take it. Inflation doesn't need to reach even close to double figures to spell disaster for the markets. The structural weaknesses in the economy will induce a massive crisis because so much depends on near-zero interest rates. Debt-to-GDP ratios around the globe have risen over the past decade, as have corporate and household debts. We all bumped along OK, because while debt ratios were high, the cost of servicing this debt was low. The second these rates need to rise it is likely to cause panic. If long-term rates have to rise by just a few percentage points, we could be looking at another crash.

Unless there are changes in the approach to the crisis, it seems highly likely that economic output will remain depressed for some time to come. The unemployment rate will probably remain stubbornly high for at least the next decade, too. Any move to remedy the situation will depend upon a broad recognition that emergency measures such as QE, furlough schemes and bail-outs won't be enough to restore economies to health. (And, don't forget, central banks may well ignore any rise in prices, at least to begin with, because inflation is a handy tool to whittle down the gigantic debt piles that governments have been racking up over the past decade or more.) The pandemic has inflicted damage on the real economy and that needs to be fixed. On past performance, any decision to revise deeply entrenched policies can't be expected soon. Previous recessions have created very little lasting change. Elected leaders have been quick to talk about wealth inequality and reining in markets when the chips were down, but once the immediate crisis was over they did very little to change the policies that supported that inequality. As a result, wealthier sections of society have been able to hunker down and then pretty much return to their previous patterns of saving and investment once things returned to normal. Each time, the reward was a long, and lasting, recovery. This time, though, it will be different. Everyone will suffer and the damage could be very long-term indeed.

Right now, it is difficult to predict exactly how different things will be and how they will play out. Exceptional factors are already in play, which will slow any recovery. During the COVID-19 crisis some have been able to reduce the massive private debts accrued in the 2008/9 crash but many haven't, and the general debt level remains high, which will depress consumption for years to come. Population ageing across the Western world will mean a shrinking working population having to support increasing numbers of retired people, which will undermine growth, while at the same time increasing the fiscal burdens on nations already saddled with massive debts thanks to the measures taken to address the pandemic. Also, we have yet to experience the negative supply-chain shocks if deglobalisation is widely adopted and starts to reveal its true cost (see Chapter Two).

What we can say is that the recovery, when it comes, won't be smooth, or uniform. It won't fit into a neat description like U-shaped, V-shaped or Z-shaped. While brief V-shapes have emerged at national level, notably in China and briefly in the USA when retail and housing sales rose to pre-crisis levels, it could be said that V stands for volatility because the situation keeps changing. To hope for a Z-shaped recovery, where the economy turns down but then bounces back above the pre-pandemic baseline as pent-up demand creates a boom, is ridiculously optimistic and most unlikely. Most likely, any recovery will follow a jagged line, as the world experiences a lengthy stop-start process, or take a K shape, where some segments of the economy recover at their own rates and others fall. In the worst possible case, the pandemic will permanently reduce GDP. All the investment that was lost during the extended crisis, the rethinking of global value chains, changes to fiscal policy and a slowdown in productivity growth could keep GDP far below past levels.

# FIVE

# Assets That Do Well In Stagflation

There is no doubt whatsoever that a prolonged period of stagflation will have a massive impact on the wider world. That said, we do all need to look out for ourselves during such turbulent times. Therefore, the big question has to be: what does it all mean for your portfolio? It is inevitable that a lengthy period of economic malaise will have a serious and material impact on long-term returns and return expectations.

How does anyone prosper in such a volatile environment? When an economy moves into stagflation the general consensus is that there are few opportunities for financial gain. At a time of uncertainty, it might be tempting to park at least some cash in a savings account and leave it there until the crisis blows over. Aside from the fact that it may be some years before this is the case, the 'do nothing' strategy will substantially erode the value of any portfolio. Fiat currency is dying and issuing money continues to erode its value. Parking cash in savings accounts will not shield anyone from the side effects of stagflation. Ignore the old adage 'turnover is vanity, profit is sanity and cash is reality'. This saying does not stand up to scrutiny right now. Relying on cash in the unprecedented aftermath of the COVID-19 pandemic will end badly. The truth is, thanks to the haphazard responses of governments and central banks to the threat of stagflation, fiat money is in serious danger. Its value is being steadily eroded and there seems no good end in sight.

Individuals need to plan their strategy carefully and diversifying is key. A good tip is to treat your finances like a small business. In other words, rather than just reacting to events and leaping into whatever strategy, or supposedly safe asset, feels right at the time, it's much better to look at all the options before things become really bad, in order to plot a safe and prosperous way ahead. Then, as we move forward, any investment strategy will involve keeping a meticulous track of revenues, spending and overhead costs. It's also useful to be constantly aware of the wider environment, including increased prices and changes to economic stimulus packages, so the strategy can be adjusted if needs be. You need to be agile.

The broad foundation of any personal investment strategy during a period of stagflation is fairly simple. Prioritise value over growth every time. Solvency is going to matter. Balance sheets are going to matter. Don't look at the here and now. Intermittent lockdowns encouraged a lot of people to adopt a here-and-now mindset, looking no further forward than, say, the next four or eight weeks. As Chapter Four pointed out, individuals talking about a V- or U-shaped recovery are not thinking this through; recovery from coronavirus is the long haul. Investors need to think in terms of a massive contraction of productivity and supply of goods for years to come.

Plenty of 'traditional' investment strategies will no longer apply. The stock market has long been a go-to option when it comes to choosing an investment vehicle that can offer returns at a margin above the inflation rate. In the early days of stagflation, this might well have looked like an obvious bet again. Issuing money and low interest rates have inflated stocks and kept the market buoyant. Looking back to the 1970s, the last time we saw stagflation, many investors learned the hard way that it is not possible to keep up with inflation by depending solely on stocks. Unemployment drags down productivity which in turn drags down the markets. In the USA, for example, which suffered a similar period of stagflation to the UK, the Consumer Price Index rose by 103% through the 1970s, while the S&P 500 (excluding dividends) only enjoyed a 16% increase.[30] No amount of money being pumped into the system can save companies whose revenue has dried up completely. What we will see is valuations of companies failing to reflect vastly diminished profit and earning streams, or reduction or cancellation of dividends. It is inevitable that sectors such as travel, leisure, retail and commercial property will get into real trouble, and many individual businesses won't be able to pull themselves out of the downturn.

Those loyal to stocks might look to large technology businesses such as Amazon and Apple, which have increasingly been seen as a sure thing by investors thanks to their dominant market position, and the potential for structural growth thanks to increasing digitalisation. Certainly, tech companies were among the biggest beneficiaries of lockdown life with widespread homeworking, consumption of online entertainment and internet shopping. Investors should, however, think carefully about growth stocks. It is not a good idea to own anything expensive in the current environment. There is a limit to how long tech stocks can defy gravity and most commentators doubt whether the numbers add up. If you took a snapshot of a basket of equal numbers of each of the 'FAANGM' stocks (Facebook, Apple, Amazon,

Netflix, Google and Microsoft) in August 2020, it had a P/E ratio of 54.6, versus 25.3 for the S&P 500. There was a price-to-sales ratio of 8 (versus 2.4) and a cyclically adjusted price-to-earnings (CAPE) ratio of a somewhat substantial 163 (versus 27.7).[31] Apple boasts the highest weight of any stock in the S&P 500 over the past four decades. When you look at the basic figures, it is hard not to think: *bubble*. It is hard to envisage these tech giants maintaining their current growth rate.

What, then, of value investing? This is the approach of buying cheap stocks in often unfashionable industries. American economists Eugene Fama and Kenneth French found that seeking out bargains, judged on the basis of comparing a business's share price to the value of its assets, in the long run can return significantly more than the broader equity market. Unfortunately, this is not the case today. In fact, value investing is suffering the worst run it's seen in two centuries.[32] This run began in the aftermath of the 2008/09 crisis and the pandemic exacerbated the trends that made some companies and sectors seem cheap or expensive. By October 2020, MSCI's index of global value stocks had fallen around 12%, which lagged far behind its growth index counterpart, which had soared by almost 22%.

Any investor determined to remain in stocks to retain some diversity in their portfolio would be advised to focus on sectors covering the fundamentals such as food, energy and shelter, because these are the basics needed for survival. Valuations are extremely cheap and they've recently got cheaper thanks to the pandemic. Some sectors of the real estate market will come under pressure during a period of stagflation, for example, but human beings will always need basic shelter.

## Active or passive?

Perhaps the most important point to note here is to take *active* control of your portfolio. Most investors tend towards a passive approach, putting the responsibility for managing funds into the hands of wealth managers. Yet, arguably, we are at the most vulnerable point for passive funds in living memory. Let me explain why.

Individuals turn to passive funds because they are simple; put your money in and set it to run to (say) your retirement date in twenty or thirty years' time. Let the 'experts' get on with it and a decent return is pretty much guaranteed. There is no need to study the fundamentals of the businesses you are invested in. However, there is a big difference between active and passive management of a portfolio. An active manager will buy a business's prospects, may sell when it reaches a benchmark and will sell if it fails to perform. A wealth manager running a passive fund *has to hold* stocks that meet the fund's criteria, because clients demand this. For example, if a fund is designed to track an index, it will usually hold the stocks that make up that index. If demand is high, the manager may need to buy more of those stocks. It's no surprise that the active investors see them coming and try to ratchet up the price. The wealth managers running passive funds have some flexibility over when to buy but must pay the going rate, unless it is significantly higher than the price ranges they set. That's concerning in any environment, but there is another reason why this approach is dangerous today. Passive strategies have grown so popular that they now eclipse active funds, accounting for almost 50% of the US market, for instance,[33] where they accounted for just 10% in 2003.[34] Think about this for a moment; these are stocks that the wealth managers have to hold. If money comes in, they may need to buy. If it goes out, they may need to sell. It is a big ask to expect the stock market to reflect the underlying fundamentals of the economy when so much of it is bought and sold (with corresponding impact on valuations) at times that might not reflect what the economy is doing.

What does this all mean to the individuals who place their trust in passive investing? Well, those active managers see the passive fund managers coming, both when they're seeking to buy and when they're trying to sell. If we reach a situation where large numbers of investors want out because, say, the market starts to fall rapidly in the aftermath of the pandemic, there will be demand for money to flow out of the passive funds. If they cannot meet this demand from money coming in, wealth managers will need to sell stock to somebody. Now, if you realise I am desperate to sell, would you pay top dollar? Probably not. Prices will inevitably be driven down. In theory, there is no limit on how low. It is conceivable that there may be no buyers at all, making some funds worthless, at least in the short term. The investors will not care that they paid the manager to track an index, if that index goes into free fall. The 'small print' may allow the fund manager to delay payment in circumstances like this, but some funds may have to declare bankruptcy. If you want to come out from the current situation unscathed, do not rely on passive funds: in the scenario I have painted, you might struggle to get your money out.

If you are alarmed by volatility in the markets, you might consider moving money into bonds. Bond markets tend not to see such big swings in value. However, be cautious about this strategy too, since they do fluctuate when interest rates change, or when the market decides a change is overdue or inadequate. This is the reason why long bonds don't look attractive in an environment of stagflation. Several prominent analysts have warned about inflation's impact on bonds. The nightmare scenario for bond investors would be soaring inflation at a time of over-supply in the market. There is going to be a lot of pressure on yields. Central banks might react by taking interest rates into negative territory, although governments are likely to resist such a move as most are shortly going to have to try to sell bonds to recover some of the pandemic deficits. The market is unlikely to buy bonds in a glutted market unless they offer attractive coupon rates or the price is heavily discounted. There is therefore the real possibility that once interest rates start going up again, they are going to shoot up, which means those holding bonds at that point will lose value: if coupon payments start to appear low the value of the bond will fall. This is also an incentive for those thinking about buying bonds to hold on in the hope of better terms.

Another possible scenario is where central banks step up QE: buy up their own debt. Technically, there is no limit to the amount of debt a central bank can buy. In Japan, the central bank owns over 40% of the outstanding bonds issued by the government. The ECB mopped up 90%

of the €2.1 trillion of debt issued by European governments in the period between March 2015 and December 2018.[35] Yet these actions were taken against a very different backdrop of low inflation. We've never been in a situation where central banks have intervened to buy up debt at a time of high inflation. It's an untried policy and could become a toxic combination for bonds. It is for this reason that some commentators warn that even a small rise in inflation could prove costly for bond investors and could wipe out a significant portion of returns.

Anyone who wants their investment portfolio to beat inflation in a tough market needs to get strategic. They need to actively consider what it is that will create balance, in a world where QE remains the only strategy available to central banks against a backdrop of rising inflation. What assets will do well in this challenging environment? Agility and diversification are probably more important than ever. With every nation around the globe shifting from interdependence to independence, the high correlation across all global assets is probably going to decline, which means the need to diversify assets globally is essential. With stagflation a real prospect, investors should start by researching the widest possible range of assets and thinking in terms of long-term valuation to assess the scope for sustainable yield. Then, once a direction of travel is identified, they should stress-test any assumptions made against the scenario of a lengthy period of stagflation.

At the time of writing, we have yet to see any real movement in inflation and all the signs are that the market remains soothed by the various efforts to keep a lid on it. Indeed, expectations of a surge in inflation were low throughout 2020, despite the turbulent economic conditions. This has kept inflation-linked bonds relatively cheap. These bonds, the principal of which is indexed to inflation (or deflation) on a daily basis, would therefore make an attractive diversifier in a broad portfolio, as well as a hedge against the corrosive impact of rising prices.

# Commodities

Commodities such as gold, oil and industrial metals would be another useful component in a diversified investment portfolio. They certainly performed well during the 1970s stagflation, returning 50% from April 1973 to December 1974, during which period stock markets lost 31%.[36] While this time around 'Big Oil' companies have taken a knock – after being adversely affected by unprecedented fall in demand, which prompted energy producers to slash dividends, rack up debt levels and sell, or write down, assets – commodity funds have so far outperformed broad stock markets even during the most intense periods of the pandemic. In the first quarter of 2020, the S&P 500 fell by about 30%, while the benchmark Bloomberg Commodity Index fell by 20% in the same timeframe.[37] This is not exactly stellar, but it does provide an indication that fundamentals might offer a safer bet.

What makes this argument in favour of commodities stronger is that there are several low-cost ways to gain exposure to these assets today, ways that simply weren't available in the 1970s. The four options available are commodity index funds, commodity-oriented exchange-traded funds (ETFs), commodity stocks and commodity futures and options. It should be noted that many funds offering direct exposure to commodities do not pay income, as they seek to add value (via price appreciation) over the investor's holding period.

Commodity index funds pool money from investors into financial instruments based on, or linked to, commodity price futures, replicating the performance of one, or several, commodity price indexes. The advantage here is liquidity, since (in normal times) investors can leave a fund rapidly, incurring only minimal transaction fees (but you should check the small print for payment deferral conditions). The long-term management fees can, however, be higher than for simple, stock market index funds, particularly among the smaller commodity index fund companies. A close cousin of commodity index funds are commodity-led exchange traded funds that invest in the stocks of oil and energy companies, gold mining enterprises, and other natural resource or agriculture operations. These give a relatively low-cost exposure to a broad basket of metals, both precious and industrial, and may include agricultural commodities as well. The advantage of a tracking fund is it is very difficult to predict the fortunes of a particular commodity – fossil fuel, say, or sugar. However, this option spreads the risk in bad times and as industry recovers tracking funds will almost certainly recover too.

It is, of course, feasible to go for a more do-it-yourself version, assembling a portfolio of commodity stocks using online discount brokerages, which charge relatively small amounts per transaction. This is an option for long-term investors, who might be keen to avoid year-on-year fund management fees. Depending on personal preferences, it is possible to assemble a diversified portfolio across different commodity sectors, thereby decreasing any risks of exposure to a particular market. Likewise, if an investor feels bullish about a single commodity, they might like to assemble their portfolio out of several stocks to avoid the impact of any setback at individual companies. Think here of an event that could deeply impact an organisation, such as the 2010 Deepwater Horizon oil spill, which saw BP paying $18.7 billion in fines and axing its dividend. An investor would obviously like to cushion themselves from that sort of fall-out.

Perhaps the most risky commodity investment is futures. This is where an investor promises to buy or sell a commodity at a given price on a future date. If investors are 'long' it means they are promising to buy at that time and the 'strike' price fixed in the contract; if 'short', they are promising to sell at that price by that date. Investors do not actually handle the physical product. Almost all futures contracts are financial obligations to be settled in cash, or sold on to someone else. To understand how this might work, imagine that oil is selling at $35 a barrel today. An investor decides to go long and commits to selling 1,000 barrels in six months' time at (say) $35 a barrel. If, at the end of that six-month period, oil is selling at $32 a barrel, the investor will gain $3 a barrel, less transaction costs. They will buy oil at $32 a barrel on that day and then immediately sell their 1,000 barrels at the strike price, netting their $3,000 profit. Obviously, if the oil price went the other way and rose to $38 a barrel, the investor would lose $3,000, plus transaction costs. Gains or losses would be even higher if prices changed more. The attraction of futures is the potential for large gains, but it is, as you can see, quite risky. This is why investors are often asked to place deposits against losses in a brokerage account. If the price starts to go heavily the wrong way, they might be asked for a top-up, too. If the investor is unable to inject more cash, the account will be closed out before the expiry date and the investor will be liable for any additional costs above the value of the deposit.

Of all commodities, a great beneficiary of stock market volatility is usually to be gold. As I explain in my book *Gold Rush 2020*, gold has a long reputation as an inflation hedge and haven from stock market downturns. It shone during the 1970s, rising from $100 in late 1976 to around $650 in 1980, when the Consumer Price Index (CPI) rate peaked in the US at 14% then fell, hovering between $350 and $450 for the next decade. The point to note here is that in a time of stagflation, gold is highly likely to gain ground. Indeed, it has already made significant gains. In August 2020, the spot price of gold hit an all-time high of $2,000 an ounce, after rising more than 32% since the beginning of the year.[38] Commentators were dubbing it a new gold rush. It has been predicted that the price could rise to $3,500 within two years, or perhaps even beyond that.[39]

Ultimately, inflation makes us all poorer, but in an inflationary environment gold attracts additional interest and market demand can drive its price up faster than inflation. Investors can buy bars of gold, or shares in firms that deal in the precious metal. It's also possible to buy shares in mining firms that extract gold, or to gain exposure to it through trading groups such as my own business, RTK International Holdings, which helps people wanting to invest in gold.

Another asset class that is expected to weather the storm fairly resiliently is property. While investment in commercial properties is regarded as increasingly risky in an environment where many large companies are shedding staff, or switching large numbers of employees into permanent homeworking, don't be too hasty to ignore the potential. There will be some down-sizing and movement away from expensive city-centre locations, but there are also signs of growth in 'urban hubs' and business parks. Many businesses have found that their employees favour a combination of home and office working, but prefer to drive short distances when they have to go to the workplace. I advise caution here: commercial property is worth considering as part of a diverse strategy, but do not become too exposed to it.

Another potential area for growth, whether as a private investor or via a global investment fund, is domestic property. UK property website Rightmove has reported a surge in people searching for homes further from towns and city centres as home owners re-evaluate their circumstances after the lockdowns. The point to remember here is that, even if the price of the average home falls, it will remain a good investment for the long term. While govern-ment bonds are paying 0.5% interest a year, a property making 3–5% looks attractive. If you don't have thousands of pounds to invest, and don't want to manage rentals, there are a number of 'fractional' opportunities to invest in domestic property, where investors can put in small sums to buy a share in a property via tokens. Highly attractive expected yields will be quoted, but treat these with caution and do your homework.

The final potential investment to highlight is Bitcoin. Bitcoin and cryptocurrencies have been much touted as an inflation-resistant hedge against a background of shrinking GDP, economic slowdown and endless QE. Digital assets are not (or at least, not so) beholden to the whims of political decision-making, and are defined by their verifiable supply. There is now a great deal of interest in Bitcoin from institutional investors as much of the data begins to suggest a forthcoming bull run. What excites many is that Bitcoin halve the number of new 'coins' being issued to 'miners' every four years. This means that Bitcoin's stock-to-flow (the number of years at the current production rate required to achieve the current supply) is increasing. It currently stands at fifty years, which is similar to gold. It is quite likely that lesser-known cryptocurrencies may fly alongside their more established big brother too. However, while there are many cryptocurrencies on the market, only a handful warrant serious consideration as an investment and potential hedge. As a rule of thumb, the smaller the market capitalisation of the crypto-asset, the higher the potential risk, although it could also be said that this goes two ways, since a higher risk ought to bring a higher reward (in a perfect market). Bitcoin and other cryptocurrencies are not entirely separate from the broader financial markets. If a crisis looms and investors need to sell what they can, Bitcoin might be the first to be put on the block. A considered viewpoint might be that Bitcoin (or equivalent) is not digital gold, and certainly not insurance, but it could be an interesting speculation.

Investors should choose their stagflation portfolio carefully because an increase in inflation, even a moderate one, will have major investment implications. This will mean limiting your exposure to assets such as government bonds and low-yielding corporate bonds which will suffer in an inflationary environment. Instead, portfolios should be made up of assets that will benefit from increased inflation. Gold usually performs well during periods of high inflation and digital currency might, this time around. Even a small rise in global demand could also lead to a surge in commodities, which were trading at very depressed levels in 2020 and are currently out of favour with investors.

# SIX

# Make More, Save More, Invest More

One of the things most people find the hardest to do is to view life's challenges in their simplest form. While the picture being painted in this book is bleak, it does not require a complex strategy to come out on top. Indeed, if you were to summarise the best way to stay ahead, the answer is simple: *make more money, save more money and invest more money.*

It took me many years to acknowledge that the way I tackle things is not the same as the way most others do. Whenever I encounter a challenge, I think like a true entrepreneur and look for the simplest possible solution. Often that solution turns out to be the most obvious path, but others discount it because it is just *too* simple. But follow this process to its logical conclusion, and look at all the best entrepreneurial ideas you've ever heard about: these are led by people who saw, and followed the obvious, before it became obvious to everyone else. I don't allow complicated processes to cloud my thoughts, or work through all the answers to all the 'what ifs'. I just look for what needs to be done and plot the shortest and easiest possible course to achieve it. The strategy I suggest might sound mind-numbingly simple, given the scale of the challenge facing us all, but believe me, this is the only way out of it.

Let's start with the basics. To get started, you need to learn how money works. It is not wise or acceptable to expect things to just happen for you when it comes to getting through the next decade. You need to take active, well-thought-through decisions about your finances. Therefore, starting right now, a thirst for more knowledge about money has to be your new hobby.

As you learn more, hopefully you will begin to completely change the way you think about money. Today the world sits on a bubble of debt that is ready to pop. I am not alone in my belief that this must change. The way we've been thinking about debt is all wrong. To not just survive, but thrive, we need to stay out of debt and save more.

Once you learn more, you can start to take action. Listed below are some ideas to get you started, according to the simple strategy I outlined here.

## Make more money

If you really mean business, it might be prudent to, well, start a business if you have not done so already. Put it this way: how many of your closest friends, family or in fact anyone you know or see in the news are super-rich *and* work for someone else? OK, there may be some, but they are the exception rather than the rule. Very often, the super-rich employees work in banks or financial services, so they know how the monetary system works and how to make money whilst working for someone else.

The point here is, if you don't yet own your own business, you might like to consider starting one in order to give your opportunity for wealth that final push. Turn that hobby, or side project, into a business and overnight you will open up opportunities to make yourself better off.

There are many advantages to running a business (and if you are already running one, these also apply to you – make sure you take advantage of all these possibilities):

## Multiple revenue streams

If all your revenue is coming from one source, what happens if they go bust, or find a cheaper supplier? Turn it around: if your income is coming from several sources, not only are you not dependent on any of them, but you now have several ways to make more money.

## Reduced tax burden

Once you own a business there are many opportunities to reduce tax liabilities. On a very basic level this means the bulk of a business owner's income can be taken via dividend payments, which are more tax-effective. This could possibly be extended, to pay a partner an annual dividend that is below the 40% tax threshold, which is £50,001 at the time of writing. It's prudent to let the rest of the company's earnings build up; then, after two or three years, the company can be liquidated and the value in it taken out. This won't avoid tax entirely. The owner of this company (you) will pay 20% tax on the final year's company profits and a 10% entrepreneur tax on the amount left in the company when it closed down. Overall though, the tax bill will be substantially smaller than if the same person had been paying income tax over the same period.

To break it down, let's look at an individual who previously enjoyed a salary of £200,000 per year. They'd be paying £75,000 a year in income tax, so the income hitting their bank account would be £125,000. If £200,000 was a company's profit, the owner would pay 19% (corporation tax) on the whole amount, which is £38,000. That director could take £50,000 out of the company as a dividend, providing that this is their only income.

If their partner did the same, they would have withdrawn £100,000 altogether, and paid £15,000 in income tax plus £38,000 in corporation tax, making £53,000. This leaves £100,000 in the company when it is liquidated, on which 10% tax is due (£10,000). In total, the company director will have paid £63,000 instead of £75,000, a saving of £12,000. By this calculation, the more you earn, the more you save.

## Maximise working capital

Take a leaf out of the book of the super-wealthy. Take a large proportion of any revenue and reinvest it back into the business, rather than paying yourself (and/or partner) a dividend in a particular year. R&D tax positively encourages innovation, even though few people seem to know about it, or understand the potential. Government schemes, which could mean tens of thousands, even hundreds of thousands, of pounds to individual businesses are woefully under-utilised. Part of the problem is the outdated assumption that R&D only applies to scientific projects, when in fact it applies to innovation in many forms across all sectors.

The government's focus is to encourage economic growth and success and therefore the definition is quite broad: while the criteria state that a project should resolve 'scientific or technological uncertainty', it can be applied to a range of work, whether it is a new process, product or service, or an improvement to an existing one. Claims have been made in sectors as varied as administration and support services, construction, transport and storage, arts, entertainment and recreation. R&D doesn't need to be successful to qualify and claims can be made two years from the end of the tax year in which the work happened.

Further afield, there are a number of tax reliefs available to encourage external corporate investment in anything from films to other businesses, and the schemes offer upfront tax relief on the investment. The Enterprise Investment Scheme (EIS) offers relief on 30% of the amount invested, up to £1 million a year (more if yours is a 'knowledge-intensive company'). If the enterprise turns a profit, the scheme can pay out a dividend each year, which may be taxed if the investor earns enough elsewhere. Some investors take out a loan to invest in the EIS and then use the dividend to repay the loan (although the government does have some strict rules about this so it is worth checking first on their website).[40] If, for example, an investor was able to borrow £1 million, they could put it into an EIS, which would produce tax relief of £300,000. There is a risk involved, which is why the government is prepared to offer tax relief, to incentivise investment. A similar concept is Venture Capital Trusts (VCTs) which also offer 30% tax relief on investments up to £200,000. VCTs are a specialist investment trust, where investments are managed by fund managers, rather than chosen by individual investors.

Charitable giving is another option. While the government has tried and failed to crack down on potential abuses of this practice, if anyone gives assets to charity, they can claim income tax relief up to the entire amount given. The government's Directgov website outlines an example of how individuals can donate a property worth £90,000 to a chosen charity and then claim tax relief for £89,900.[41] Obviously, this will mean that the donor loses the asset, but they will be reducing taxable income substantially. This opens up the potential to reduce taxable income to zero if enough is given away. There is also an alternative option, which allows the investor to keep hold of the asset and still reduce tax liabilities. Here, anyone with a freehold property can grant a lease on it and give that lease to their chosen charity. If, say, the lease was for a six-year term, the charity would hold the property for the lease period and benefit from any rental income during that time. At the end of the term, the property would revert to the owner. While there won't be any tax relief on the value of the freehold, the tax relief on the lease is still worth having. If the property is in London, property owners could be looking at tax relief into five figures.

## Mergers and acquisitions

The start-up phase of any small business is inherently challenging, which is why my strategy has long been to buy ready-made businesses with an existing management team and clients and then to merge them into my existing portfolio. Existing businesses already have the infrastructure that many start-ups are tying themselves in knots to build. There are a large number of businesses for sale at the moment and that number will grow as the economy tightens. These businesses don't necessarily have inherent or underlying problems, they may simply have run out of money in the current environment; but as with any major purchase, don't skimp your homework.

There is another rich pool of M&A opportunity worth exploring that has very little to do with the fall-out of the pandemic. We are in the midst of a baby boomer retirement boom. This is the generation that was born immediately after the Second World War, who have boosted the economy by working longer than many previous generations. According to some surveys, the majority of current small businesses were started and run by this generation, too. In fact, over the past quarter of a century, three times as many baby boomers decided to start their own businesses between 1995 and 2015 as did so between 1970 and 1995.[42] In the USA, for example, there are 12 million baby boomer small or medium-sized enterprises, with $10 trillion of assets.[43] Now though, boomers across the globe are lining up to look for the exit. In 2019, over 31% of the UK population were aged 55 or above and, for those who followed their own entrepreneurial path, their nest egg is tied up in the business they've built over their lifetimes.[44] Baby boomer business owners may need to sell if they need the proceeds for their retirement. I suspect many will now be actively looking for an exit because of the pandemic. For a careful and well-informed buyer there are bound to be substantial opportunities.

The obvious objection is: lack of funds. How will you afford to buy a business? Well, raising money and buying a business is a lot easier than you think. It is perfectly possible to raise money in a variety of ways just as you would in any business venture and, of course, you may be able use the value of the business you are buying as collateral. It should be mentioned that access to capital may be reduced if the economy is under severe pressure, which could reduce options in the M&A market. However, if the businesses you will be targeting have an established track record (as, over time, so will you), you've got something solid to talk to investors about.

## Pay yourself first

This may seem a granny-suck-eggs moment, but if you follow any of these business strategies, don't forget the golden rule: pay yourself first. Most business owners get this part wrong. You start a business to put more money in your own pocket, so do so. Pay yourself a salary automatically, just as you would with every other member of staff.

This piece of advice leads me to the second part of the simple strategy:

# Save more money

Treat your own personal finances with the same care and attention that you would give to any business accounts. Aside from the fact that it is crucial to know where you are, it's often easier to *save* money than to *make* fresh reserves of money. To this end, there are a number of easy housekeeping steps that should become part of your normal routine.

## Automate your savings

Set up a process to sweep a set amount of savings into a separate account on a regular basis. If you don't need to think about it, then it will soon become a habit.

## Create genuine accountability

Create a detailed financial plan with a monthly or weekly budget. By creating these simple documents it is easy to see whether they are both reasonable and achievable. Once you've gone through this process, don't just put it away and forget about it. You are the person that is responsible for making it happen. Don't look to others if your plan doesn't go as expected.

## Don't underestimate your needs

If you don't allow yourself the things you are used to, or really need or want, you will soon break your budget and start making excuses.

Be reasonable. If you are new to saving, start slowly. This part needs real commitment.

## Be in it for the long haul

When things start to get better, don't allow yourself to get distracted. These tough times are set to endure for a while to come. Anyone who falls into the trap of letting their lifestyle choices dominate the financial controls they've put in place could quickly find their well-laid plans unravelling at an alarming rate. Patience and commitment are the key to success. The final part of the strategy is to:

# Invest more money

In today's financial world every type of investment has become far more accessible to the average person. In Chapter Five, we looked at all of the various possibilities on offer and I would urge everyone to find out as much as possible about each one. My love of investing grew and grew, the more knowledge I gained, and so did my successes. Knowledge is power. Do your homework so you understand what you are investing in, the likely risk, the potential reward and the possibility of failure. Investing is like gambling: most people don't win but the experts do. Expertise comes from knowledge.

If you are going it alone, some tips to bear in mind:

**Don't invest too much money upfront.** Use an agile approach. Test, measure, change.

**Don't underestimate the timeline.** Don't bank on everything going to plan every time. If you have an exit plan, make sure you assume it will take longer to meet your goals, and that the returns will be lower, than your first figures suggest. That way you should usually overdeliver on your financial plans.

**Don't copy other people.** Your plan is for your future. Everyone has different aspirations regarding what they want and what they need. Understand your own wants and needs and then build a plan to match and achieve them.

Stagflation may appear to represent an extreme risk, and this may well be the case for many people. It is also true that most of us have never experienced an economic phenomenon like it. Likewise, we don't currently know how the authorities will respond and what changes they make to, say, the tax relief opportunities outlined here. However, while no one can predict exactly what will happen, it pays to be prepared. Get ahead of the curve and consider what stagflation, and any potential fiscal response, will do to your portfolio.

**Above all, get involved!** The greatest risk of all is doing nothing. Understand what you are investing in and why. Don't be passive, or allow other people to make your decisions for you. You will not succeed if you play the willing spectator. There are so many opportunities when it comes to creating a diversified portfolio, and even more so today with real estate and gold being fractionalised on blockchain technology, along with better access to stocks and shares, crowdfunding for private equity and more. As I said at the start of this book, fortune favours the prepared. So, do your preparation and make that fortune.

# Afterword

Even the most eternal optimist would have to admit that it is inevitable that we are heading into some tough economic times. Although the outlook for the coronavirus vaccine programme looks promising, repairing the widespread damage caused by the COVID-19 pandemic is not going to be a quick or simple process. It is a sad fact that many of the businesses that were forced to close their doors during the extended lockdowns won't be coming back. Many more companies that managed to limp through the crisis, large and small, face a tough road ahead towards any sort of meaningful recovery and may need to entirely change their business models to recover, which will lead to an increasing move towards digitalisation. This will leave millions of people unemployed and many of those that do stay in work may be forced to accept new, less steady, terms. Meanwhile, the disruption to the supply chains has been a huge shock to productivity. Take all of this together and the limited supply of skilled labour and production will create inflationary pressures. Plus, after lengthy periods of isolation and social distancing, which have led to the cancellation of numerous events, decimated the travel industry and closed restaurants and shopping centres, the scrabble to resume life as usual will very probably create negative demand shock.

In the short term, we can expect emergency lending programmes and QE to continue adding the liquidity to keep things flowing. Money will keep on being issued at a faster rate than in previous recessions, acting as a stark reminder of the seriousness of the situation, but these measures are running out of road. It doesn't help matters, either, that policymakers' attention continues to be distracted by political manoeuvring in an increasingly polarised world. Thus, many of the measures taken won't put people back into work and could well hinder, rather than help, the inflation problem. The failure to properly deal with the financial crisis of 2008/9 will further reduce the opportunities for central banks to come up with any meaningful policies. Then, even if the economic situation is somehow soothed far quicker than anyone dares to hope for, it will not be the time to breathe a sigh of relief. COVID-19 is not a one-off. In recent years we've seen a series of epidemics and pandemics: HIV since the 1980s, SARS in 2003, H1N1 in 2009, MERS in 2011 and Ebola between 2014 and 2016. Each is, essentially, man-made, born of poor health, the abuse of the natural environment and the ever-increasing interconnection of the world. Scientists are convinced the next epidemic, possibly even another pandemic, is just around the corner. Global warming and the damage we have wreaked on the planet, and continue to wreak, means these occurrences will become more common in the years ahead. With little time to recover between one global event and the next, we could all be looking at paying a very big price indeed for our failure to get properly to grips with previous crises.

All the warning signs point to a prolonged period of stagflation, which could well be very different from any economic circumstance anyone has experienced for more than forty years, with an entirely new set of outcomes. What happens next and how individual nations choose to deal with the ensuing fall-out remains to be seen. The fact is, though, with many central banks still seeming determined to stick to 'tried and tested' formulas, any sort of recovery should be expected to be slow and uneven. Prices will remain volatile, unemployment may continue to rise and there may be widespread social unrest. In such uncertain times, the onus will be on individuals to protect themselves and their assets.

Everyone should review their investment portfolios, adjust to the 'new normal' and get involved. Even if central banks don't change their tactics and find new approaches to maintain growth, we must. This will involve actively trying some entirely new strategies and reducing exposure to assets that may have been reliable in the past. Diversification is key. As comfortable as you may have grown in one sector, it won't be enough. Consider each of the opportunities outlined in this book and look to engage with as many as you can. There are plenty of opportunities in commodities, especially gold, and in cryptocurrency, inflation-linked bonds and futures.

Most of all, you need to remain agile. Don't get tied up in just one or two large bets. Think about buying into tokenised assets, which will give you the freedom to spread yourself more widely. That way if, say, the property market reacts in a way you didn't expect, you should be able to move your money elsewhere.

Meanwhile, as well as investing more, look at strategies to help you make more and save more. Maximise the wealth you have and look to reduce tax liabilities, to take advantage of opportunities governments offer. To survive, and even thrive, during a prolonged period of stagflation, adopt the billionaire mindset and reinvest your money in order to make every pound count. The future is not pretty, but with some prudent planning now, it will be possible to weather the storm of what will be the toughest economic environment for decades. Do it right and you may even come out the other side stronger than before.

# References

1 Phil Taylor-Guck, *Gold Rush 2020: Why the time to invest in gold is right now* (Rethink Press, 2019).

2 Emily Hardy, 'The last time unemployment was this low was 1974', This is Money, 24 June 2019, www.thisismoney .co.uk/money/news/article-7150007/What-life-like-1970s -Britain-time-unemployment-low.html, accessed 6 April 2021.

3 Trading Economics, 'United Kingdom Unemployment Rate', https://tradingeconomics.com/united-kingdom /unemployment-rate, accessed 6 April 2021.

4 Office for National Statistics, 'Employment, unemployment and economic inactivity', www.ons .gov.uk/employmentandlabourmarket/peopleinwork /employmentandemployeetypes/bulletins/ uklabourmarket/september2020#employment -unemployment-and-economic-inactivity, accessed 6 April 2021.

5 Ben King, 'Unemployment rate: how many people are out of work?', BBC News, 23 March 2021, www.bbc.co.uk /news/business-52660591, accessed 6 April 2021.

6 Phillip Inman, 'UK jobless rate "could near 15% in second coronavirus wave"', *The Guardian*, Business, 7 July 2020, www.theguardian.com/business/2020/jul/07/uk-jobless -rate-coronavirus-oecd-unemployment, accessed 6 April 2021.

7 Department for Work and Pensions, 'UK sees record employment as unemployment falls below 4 per cent', press release 19 March 2019, www.gov.uk/government /news/uk-sees-record-employment-as-unemployment- falls-below-4-per-cent, accessed 6 April 2021.

8  Andrew Soergel, 'Fed official warns of 30% unemployment', *U.S. News*, 23 March 2020, www.usnews.com/news /economy/articles/2020-03-23/fed-official-unemployment -could-hit-30-as-coronavirus-slams-economy, accessed 6 April 2021.

9  Harry Kretchmer, 'How coronavirus has hit employment in G7 economies', World Economic Forum, 13 May 2020, www.weforum.org/agenda/2020/05/coronavirus -unemployment-jobs-work-impact-g7-pandemic, accessed 6 April 2021.

10  Richard Partington, 'Gig economy in Britain doubles, accounting for 4.7 million workers', *The Guardian*, 28 June 2019, www.theguardian.com/business/2019/jun/28/gig -economy-in-britain-doubles-accounting-for-47-million -workers, accessed 6 April 2021.

11  Ed Peters, 'Coronavirus Crisis: Deflation, Inflation or Stagflation?', First Quadrant, April 2020, www .firstquadrant.com/system/files/2020_06_Coronavirus _Crisis_Deflation_Inflation_or_Stagflation.pdf, accessed 22 April 2021.

12  Stephen Roach, 'A return to 1970s stagflation is only a broken supply chain away', *Financial Times*, 6 May 2020, www.ft.com/content/5f4ef4f6-8ad6-11ea-a109 -483c62d17528, accessed 22 April 2021.

13  Global Agenda Council on the Global Trade System, 'The Shifting Geography of Global Value Chains: implications for developing countries and trade policy' (World Economic Forum, 2012), www3.weforum.org/docs/WEF _GAC_GlobalTradeSystem_Report_2012.pdf, accessed 7 April 2021.

14  Jon Excell, 'Last week's poll: will pandemic drive reshoring of UK manufacturing?', *The Engineer*, 5 May 2020, www.theengineer.co.uk/poll-pandemic-reshoring-uk -manufacturing/, accessed 7 April 2020.

15  Roberto Azevêdo, 'Trade set to plunge as COVID-19 pandemic upends global economy', press release 8 April 2020, www.wto.org/english/news_e/pres20_e/pr855 _e.htm, accessed 7 April 2021.

16  Douglas Irwin, 'The pandemic adds momentum to the deglobalisation trend', Vox[EU]/CEPR, 2020, https://voxeu .org/article/pandemic-adds-momentum-deglobalisation -trend, accessed 7 April 2021.

17  Bloomberg, 'Japan sets aside ¥243.5 billion to help firms shift
    production out of China', *The Japan Times*, 9 April 2020,
    www.japantimes.co.jp/news/2020/04/09/business/japan
    -sets-aside-¥243-5-billion-help-firms-shift-production
    -china/#.XqXRyVNKiu4, accessed 7 April 2021.

18  Raphael Auer, Claudio Borio and Andrew Filardo, 'The
    Globalisation of Inflation: the growing importance of
    global value chains', Bank for International Settlements
    Working Paper No. 602, 2017, www.bis.org/publ/work602
    .pdf, accessed 7 April 2021.

19  Nuffield Foundation, 'COVID-19 pandemic could increase
    youth unemployment by 600,000 this year', press release
    6 May 2020, www.nuffieldfoundation.org/news/covid-19
    -pandemic-could-increase-youth-unemployment-by-600000
    -this-year, accessed 7 April 2021.

20  Aegon, 'Baby Boomers Hotspots Report 2019', www.aegon
    .co.uk/content/dam/ukpaw/hidden/baby-boomer-report
    -2019.pdf, accessed 7 April 2021.

21  Andre Belelieu and Yvonne Sonsino, 'Coronavirus is
    creating retirement insecurity', World Economic Forum,
    2020, www.weforum.org/agenda/2020/08/here-are-10
    -steps-to-diffuse-the-timebomb-of-an-ageing-population
    -post-covid19, accessed 7 April 2021.

22  Bank of England, 'What is quantitative easing?', updated
    5 November 2020, www.bankofengland.co.uk/monetary
    -policy/quantitative-easing, accessed 7 April 2020.

23  Ben King, 'What is quantitative easing and how will it
    affect you?', BBC News, 5 November 2020, www.bbc.co.uk
    /news/business-15198789, accessed 7 April 2021.

24  Polly Curtis, 'Reality check: does quantitative easing
    work?', *The Guardian* Politics Blog, 6 October 2011, www
    .theguardian.com/politics/reality-check-with-polly-curtis
    /2011/oct/06/reality-check-does-quantitative-easing-work,
    accessed 7 April 2021.

25  University of Sydney, 'Socio-economic, environmental
    impacts of coronavirus quantified', press release, 10 July
    2020, available at www.sydney.edu.au/news-opinion
    /news/2020/07/10/socioeconomic-and-environmental
    -impacts-of-coronavirus-quantifie.html, accessed 7 April
    2021.

26  Ryan Morrison, 'Covid-19 pandemic has cost the world's
    economy $3.8TRILLION "and made 147 million
    people unemployed" study claims', *Daily Mail Online*,

www.dailymail.co.uk/sciencetech/article-8506463/Covid-19-pandemic-cost-worlds-economy-3-8TRILLION.html, accessed 22 April 2021.

27 Rob Morgan, 'The news is bad – so why is the stock market buoyant?', Charles Stanley, News, 25 June 2020, www.charles-stanley.co.uk/group/cs-live/news-bad---so-why-stock-market-buoyant, accessed 8 April 2021.

28 Andrew Walker, 'Coronavirus: UK economy could be among worst hit of leading nations, says OECD', BBC News, 10 June 2020, www.bbc.co.uk/news/business-52991913, accessed 8 April 2021.

29 Cliff d'Arcy, 'British misery index hits 19-year high!', loveMONEY.com, 6 November 2011, www.lovemoney.com/news/13268/british-misery-index-hits-19year-high, accessed 8 April 2021.

30 Craig Blanchfield, 'How to prepare your portfolio for stagflation', Seeking Alpha.com, 10 August 2018, https://seekingalpha.com/article/4197655-how-to-prepare-your-portfolio-for-stagflation, accessed 8 April 2021.

31 Sebastian Mullins, '20% in 2020: how long can tech stocks defy gravity?', Schroders, 10 August 2020, www.schroders.com/en/au/institutions/insights/real-matters/20-in-2020-how-long-can-tech-stocks-defy-gravity/, accessed 8 April 2021.

32 Robin Wigglesworth and Naomi Rovnick, 'Covid condemns value investing to worst run in two centuries', *Financial Times*, 26 October 2020, www.ft.com/content/fc7ce313-92f8-4f51-902b-f883afc1e035, accessed 8 April 2021.

33 John Gittelsohn, 'End of era: passive equity funds surpass active in epic shift', Bloomberg, 11 September 2019, www.bloomberg.com/news/articles/2019-09-11/passive-u-s-equity-funds-eclipse-active-in-epic-industry-shift, accessed 8 April 2021.

34 George Gammon, 'Passive investing bubble: is YOUR retirement in danger? (Yes! Here's why)', posted on YouTube, 20 August 2020, www.youtube.com/watch?v=2Y8k73E1K4A&feature=youtu.be, accessed 8 April 2021.

35 Marcello Minenna, 'The legacy of the ECB's bond buying program', *Financial Times*, 7 May 2019, https://ftalphaville.ft.com/2019/05/07/1557223379000/The-legacy-of-the-ECB-s-bond-buying-program/, accessed 8 April 2021.

36 This is Money, 'How investors can beat "stagflation"', 10 February 2011, www.thisismoney.co.uk/money/investing /article-1712335/How-investors-can-beat-stagflation.html, accessed 22 April 2021.

37 Benjamin Cole, 'The commodity triple play in the midst of the COVID-19 economy', *Real Assets Adviser*, 7(5) (2020), n.p., https://irei.com/publications/article/commodity -triple-play-midst-covid-19-economy/, accessed 8 April 2021.

38 Giles Coghlan, 'Investors are flocking to gold amid COVID-19', *Financial Times Adviser*, 12 August 2020, www.ftadviser .com/investments/2020/08/12/investors-are-flocking-to -gold-amid-covid-19, accessed 9 April 2021. It seems a good time to mention that the title of my first book was *Gold Rush 2020, Why the time to invest in gold is right now* (ReThink Press, 2019): before the pandemic.

39 Abigail Ng and Eustance Huang, 'Gold prices could hit $3,500 in two years, analyst says', 28 July 2020, www.cnbc .com/2020/07/28/gold-prices-could-hit-3500-in-two-years -analyst-says.html, accessed 22 April 2021.

40 HMRC, 'HS341 Enterprise Investment Scheme – Income Tax Relief (2019)', updated 6 April 2021, www.gov.uk /government/publications/enterprise-investment-scheme -income-tax-relief-hs341-self-assessment-helpsheet/hs341 -enterprise-investment-scheme-income-tax-relief-2019 accessed 6 May 2021.

41 HMRC, 'Calculate the value of your donation to charity', www.gov.uk/guidance/calculate-the-value-of-your -donation-to-charity, accessed 12 April 2021.

42 https://finance.yahoo.com/news/57-small-business -owners-over-215000507.html May 13, 2019.

43 California Association of Business Brokers, 'Baby boomers: incredible numbers are buying and selling businesses (part 1 of 2)', undated, https://cabb.org/news /baby-boomers-incredible-numbers-are-buying-and -selling-businesses-part-1-2, accessed 12 April 2021.

44 Aegon, 'Baby Boomers Hotspots Report 2019', https:// www.aegon.co.uk/content/dam/ukpaw/hidden/baby -boomer-report-2019.pdf, accessed 6 May 2021.

# Acknowledgements

This book is the result of me asking a lot of wise people questions and I would like to thank them all for their patience. In particular, there is Neil Barrett, my business partner in our group, RTK International Holdings. He has been unwavering in his support and, like me, is always eager to continually challenge the norm and to question whether what we are told is really the best thing for us.

Nat McLay, one of my best friends, lives on the other side of the world to me, in Australia, but is also regularly on hand to give me his view from an Australian economic perspective. Nat is a General Manager at Device Technologies, a firm which distributes technologically advanced medical equipment and consumables. He has therefore also been a great source of medical advice, especially during COVID-19. The stats that he is privy to, ahead of me and others, have allowed me to make better judgements.

Teena Lyons is my editor, friend and another source of information around COVID-19 thanks to her partner, a director at London School of Hygiene and Tropical Medicine. Without you none of this would be possible.

Thanks also to Steve Laidlaw and Brit Pearce, business partners who have listened without laughing and given me the confidence to deliver what I've learned to our entire client base. Plus, of course, I am grateful to my many clients on the other end of that delivery, who have endured my repeated pronouncements about how we all need to educate ourselves and generations thereafter to achieve better financial literacy.

Finally, a large and sincere vote of thanks go to my family. Firstly, my wife Claire, for putting up with the hours I pour into learning this stuff and for willingly giving her time to listen to me digest and regurgitate what I've learned. She has always given me her 100% support and the space to love what I do. To my children, Niamh and Max. My biggest hope is that I can be a great teacher to you. I want to educate you and help you become financially literate so that you can make better choices for your future and the generations that follow. You are the most important thing to me and no amount of money and knowledge can equal the amazing time I've spent with you throughout lockdown. You are two wonderful little people that make my heart sing. I feel the ultimate privilege being your dad and, every day, I hope that I can continue to be the best version of myself and in turn be the best dad to you.

# The Author

Phil Taylor-Guck's career has been fuelled by curiosity. After starting out in partnership with his dad in a flooring business, Phil, known as PTG, quickly discovered an entrepreneurial flair and an insatiable curiosity about finding better ways to do things. His ideas helped quickly expand the business and he moved on to create his own supply chain and new technology to expand business opportunities. This led PTG on to creating his own investment group and, since doing that, he has invested in international companies which work in technology, venture capital, private equity and real estate. A hunger to learn more about commodities, and the technology around the process of delivering them, led him to scrutinise the world of finance; a sector he concluded was riddled with serious flaws. Phil is now CEO of RTK International Holdings, a financial service and commodities trading group, spanning four continents and headquartered in Hong Kong.

⊕ www.rtkinternational.com
⊕ http://taylor-guck.co.uk
🐦 @philtaylorguck

# Praise for previous books by PTG

'The author screams experience and
seems to let out a lot of trade secrets
which is great for the reader.'
    – Amazon five-star review

'A solid resource.'
    – Amazon five-star review

'A damn good read.'
    – Amazon five-star review

Made in the USA
Coppell, TX
08 April 2022

76243108R00085